Engaging in Transnational Education

CRITICAL PRACTICE IN HIGHER EDUCATION

Acknowledgements

My thanks, as ever, go to Dr Chidochangu Mpamhanga for his ongoing support, encouragement and patience. I extend my thanks to my critical friends, Professor Ian McNay, Dr Raj Dass and Dr Sally Alsford, for their feedback on a draft of this book, and Solomon Papadopoulos and Julia Morris, whose feedback helped shape my initial proposal. And finally, thank you to the other authors in this series, Dr Catherine Bovill, Professor Joy Jarvis and Karen Clark, who joined me on this journey and provided collegiality, camaraderie and cake.

Dedication

This book is dedicated to my children, Panashe and Cecilia. May you also have opportunities to experience the kinds of rich and varied transnational encounters that have shaped my life.

Engaging in Transnational Education

Karen Smith

Series Editors: Joy Jarvis and Karen Smith

CRITICAL PRACTICE IN HIGHER EDUCATION

First published in 2020 by Critical Publishing Ltd.

British Library Cataloguing in Publication Data
A CIP record for this book is available from the British Library

ISBN: 9781913063733

This book is also available in the following e-book formats:
MOBI ISBN: 9781913063740
EPUB ISBN: 9781913063757
Adobe e-book ISBN: 9781913063764

Cover design by Out of House Limited
Text design by Greensplash Limited
Project Management by Newgen Publishing UK
Printed and bound in the UK by 4edge, Essex

Critical Publishing
3 Connaught Road
St Albans
AL3 5RX

www.criticalpublishing.com

Paper from responsible sources

Contents

Meet the **author and series editors**

 **Karen Smith** is Reader in Higher Education in the School of Education at the University of Hertfordshire. She has a strong research interest in transnational education, notably in flying faculty models and is author of the *Transnational Education Toolkit* for the Higher Education Academy. Karen spent many years working on lecturer development programmes and is now the Director of the University of Hertfordshire's Professional Doctorate in Education. Karen also leads collaborative research and development in her School, where she engages in externally funded research and evaluation and supports the development of scholarly educational practice through practitioner research.

 **Joy Jarvis** is currently Professor of Educational Practice at the University of Hertfordshire and a UK National Teaching Fellow. She has experience in a wide range of education contexts and works to create effective learning experiences for students and colleagues. She is particularly interested in the professional learning of those engaged in educational practice in higher education settings and has undertaken a range of projects, working with colleagues locally, nationally and internationally, to develop practice in teaching and leadership of teaching. Joy works with doctoral students exploring aspects of educational practice and encourages them to be adventurous in their methodological approaches and to share their findings in a range of contexts to enable practice change.

Book summary

This book offers a clear and concise introduction to transnational education (TNE). Drawing on research, current sector guidance and policy, the book asks critical questions about the role and nature of TNE; the different motivations for engaging in it; how TNE is quality assured; the profile of TNE students and their experiences; and the range of practitioners who engage in TNE. Aimed at higher education practitioners, the book draws on examples from research and practice and asks readers to consider these in relation to their own roles and contexts. TNE is practised in many different ways; this book seeks to unpack some of these differences and their inherent complexity in an accessible and engaging way.

Reviews

Having spent my time researching practitioner (both host and overseas) interactions in TNE, I passionately believe that practitioner engagement and participation is fundamental to the successful delivery of any TNE initiative. I am therefore delighted to endorse this book and recommend it to any practitioner who wishes to understand the phenomenon of TNE in greater detail to improve their knowledge and practice. It provides practitioners who are new to TNE with a concise and informed introduction to the challenges and nuances of TNE working. Moreover, it affords more experienced faculty the ability to stop and reflect on practice, encapsulated in the form of 'critical issues' and 'critical questions for practice'. A clear rationale for each chapter is provided throughout, with relevant summaries and useful texts to supplement further reading. This is an engaging and necessary read for anyone who is passionate about delivering exceptional, rewarding and collaborative TNE with colleagues for the benefit of international societies, communities and students.

Dr Claudia M Bordogna,
Senior Lecturer,
Nottingham Business School, NTU

Karen Smith has produced a highly engaging introduction to the complex field of transnational education, aimed at supporting staff working in a variety of roles to critically reflect on their understanding of TNE and how this impacts upon their pedagogy. Transnational education is unusual in the fact that staff are often isolated and lacking a community of practice with which they can readily turn to for challenge and advice. This book will appeal to those, and is set to make a positive contribution to enhancing the experiences of both staff and students across the world participating in the fast evolving forms of transnational education.

Dr Joan O' Mahony,
Senior Advisor (Learning & Teaching),
Advance HE

Chapter 1

Introduction to transnational higher education

Introduction

Internationalisation and transnational education

For many years now, there has been a strong drive in higher education towards internationalisation. There are many reasons for this increased interest and engagement in internationalisation that can be broadly categorised as social/cultural (eg developing intercultural understandings); political (eg making strategic alliances); academic (eg building reputation); and economic (eg generating income) (de Wit, 2002). Attempts to internationalise have been aided by developments in information technology, mass participation and increased demand for higher education globally, changes in higher education funding, and the mobility of people (eg students) and expertise (Campbell and van der Wende, 2000).

But what exactly is internationalisation? Leading academic in the field, Jane Knight, provides the following definition.

Internationalisation at the national, sector, and institutional levels is defined as the process of integrating an international, intercultural, or global dimension into the purpose, functions or delivery of postsecondary education

(Knight, 2003, p 2)

This integration can relate to a whole range of aspects of higher education practice, including research, enterprise, local community engagement or regional development. Its remit, then, is large. In this book, however, I narrow the focus, and concentrate on the internationalisation of student education.

The internationalisation of student education is itself also rather broad. It can refer to the movement of students; eg students studying abroad for their degrees, or students engaging in overseas exchanges, such as Erasmus. Internationalisation can also occur within the curriculum, which might include the incorporation of global case studies, alternative ways of thinking, and international fieldwork in degree programmes. Another aspect of internationalisation is transnational education (TNE), which is the focus of this book.

TNE, although only one aspect of the internationalisation agenda, is becoming increasingly important for individuals, institutions, the higher education sector, individual countries, and geographical regions alike. TNE is no longer a niche activity for a small number of academics, in the select universities of a limited number of countries. The growth of TNE, its global spread and its increasing strategic significance, institutionally and nationally, means that many more higher education practitioners are now involved, in some way, in TNE ventures. These TNE-focused roles are not just as teachers on transnational programmes, but also recruiters, programme administrators, international partnership leads, managers with responsibility for collaborative provision, international work, and quality assurance and enhancement. These different roles will all see and experience TNE differently. My experiences of TNE, for example, are as someone who has taught on TNE programmes, travelling to the host country for short, intensive teaching blocks ('flying faculty'), as a researcher of TNE teachers' experiences and quality assurance procedures, and as a developer of support materials and guidance for those engaged in TNE. My view of TNE will not be the same as someone who works as a link tutor for an international collaboration, a local tutor or an academic based at an international branch campus, for example.

This book introduces the complex field to those higher educational professionals who find themselves engaged in transnational education work, whether that is through personal interest, job remit or institutional mission. This is not, however, a 'how-to guide'; there are other publications (eg my own *Transnational Education Toolkit* Smith, 2017; Dunn and Wallace, 2008) and websites that try to do this. Nor is it a broad overview of the current higher education landscape. Rather, this book poses critical questions about the practice of TNE and invites you to reflect on them in light of your own experiences, situation and motivations. Your own experiences will stand alongside the portrayals of TNE from other practitioners, in the research literature, and in the sector guidance that is available. With such a broad and complicated topic, I can only hope to touch on some of the key questions and challenges that TNE practice presents; therefore, I will guide you to further reading to develop some of the areas raised in this book.

What I hope is that after reading this book and engaging with the material, you will have a better understanding of what TNE means for you and your higher education practice.

This first, introductory chapter looks at the following questions.

> » How is TNE defined, what else is it called, and what does that mean for practice?

» What does TNE encompass and how do different TNE models impact on staff and students?

» How has TNE developed, what are its current trends and what might happen in the future?

Transnational higher education: what's in a name?

Let's start at the very beginning with what we call this aspect of internationalisation. I have chosen transnational education, which is abbreviated to TNE or sometimes TNHE when there is an emphasis on higher education activity. In everyday language, as shown in the Oxford English Dictionary, 'transnational' is defined as *'extending or operating across national boundaries'* and transnational education is, indeed, associated with mobility and movement. Higher education has always been mobile, mobile in the sense of the *'movement of ideas, information, people, providers, technology, curricula, values and knowledge'* (Knight, 2005, p 3). When the term 'transnational education' was initially used in Australia, it was used as a differentiator between those international students who came to Australia (international students) to study and those who studied for Australian degrees outside of Australia (transnational students) (Knight, 2005). This understanding of TNE is explicit in one of the most frequently cited definitions of TNE, which comes from UNESCO/Council of Europe, where TNE is defined as:

All types of higher education study programmes or sets of courses of study, or educational services, (including those of distance education) in which the learners are located in a different country from the one where the awarding institution is based.

(UNESCO/Council of Europe, 2000, p 2)

Here the emphasis is on the location of the learner and the degree-awarding institution. The emphasis is not on the mobility of students (as in the definition of international students given above), although some students will travel to engage in TNE; or researchers; or of academic staff (as in transnational academic mobility; see Kim, 2010), although staff do sometimes travel to teach on transnational programmes (eg flying faculty teachers); but rather on the international movement of programmes and providers. Even with this narrowing of definition, as Knight has noted (2005), there is no universally accepted definition of TNE and countries, associations and agencies will adopt definitions that *'make sense from their perspective'* (Knight, 2005, p 21). Other definitions from different institutions may well place the emphasis elsewhere and attach different meanings to the same term. Or, they might not even use the term TNE at all.

There are three other terms that are either used interchangeably or instead of trans-national education (Knight, 2005).

1. Offshore education, focusing on where the student is located.
2. Borderless education, emphasising a breaking down of borders (geograph-ical, conceptual, disciplinary).
3. Cross-border education, highlighting traversing national boundaries.

Each term carries subtle differences that can result in different conceptualisations of what programme and provider mobility is, though these differences might well be lost when the terms are used interchangeably or uncritically.

Critical questions for practice

» What term or terms do you use to describe programme and provider mobility and how are those terms defined?

» Do you feel that everyone in your setting understands TNE in the same way?

» Do your international partners have the same understanding of what is meant by TNE?

Do the proliferation of terms and the nuances of meaning matter? Well, they do to a certain extent. Without a common understanding of terminology, it is difficult to know whether we are talking about the same thing. This lack of semantic precision is particularly difficult when operating cross-culturally, where language difficulties might already be present; when regulating and quality assuring transnational educa-tion; and when collecting and monitoring data on the scale and scope of transnational education. In order to overcome this '*TNE terminology chaos*', Knight and McNamara (2017, p 1), propose the term '*international programme and provider mobility (IPPM)*' to clarify and simplify what transnational education involves and to provide a single universally accepted nomenclature.

In this book, however, I continue to use transnational education and TNE to refer to international programme and provider mobility, while recognising the difficulties of its definition and reminding you that TNE activities might go under other names. If this is not already complicated enough, the terminological complexity of the umbrella term is replicated in the description of the types of activity that TNE encompasses.

What does TNE encompass? Are we talking about the same things?

There are many types of provision that fall under the umbrella of TNE. You may already be familiar with joint degrees, top-up degree programmes or validation activities through your work with collaborative partners in your own country. In TNE, this kind of provision is also present, but with a transnational element and different challenges. Other provision is more associated with TNE, eg flying faculty.

In the next section, I look at approaches to the delivery of TNE. While there are other classifications, I use the three broad delivery models outlined by HEGlobal (2016, p 45) to introduce and show some of the differences in terms of delivery and the types of provision associated with them.

TNE delivery models

Distance/online models

Associated terms: online learning; distance learning; MOOCs

In distance/online models of TNE, students are located away from the higher educa-tion provider. The students can be supported through the provision of textbooks, audio and visual materials (eg in the traditional UK Open University model) or more likely through internet-based methods within virtual learning environments (including Massive Open Online Courses [MOOCs]). Students and staff are unlikely to meet face to face and the students can be situated anywhere in the world.

Local partnership delivery models

Associated terms: franchise programme, articulation, validation programme, top-up degree, twinning arrangement, articulation, joint degree, dual degree, multiple degree

There is much variation in practice in relation to local partnership delivery models and that variation depends on the contractual arrangements drawn up between the degree-awarding institution and the local provider. In a franchise arrangement, the degree-awarding institution licenses the franchised institution to offer a degree that is substantially the same as the original (Healey, 2013, p 9). The franchise model has been a particularly popular approach to TNE in the UK. In validation arrangements, the TNE partner develops and delivers its own programme, which is validated by the degree-awarding institution (Healey, 2013, p 9). The focus here is on the quality of the programme and whether it meets the standards of the degree-awarding institution. For this reason, this approach is sometimes termed a quality assurance programme. The franchising or validating can refer to whole programmes, or to parts of them. In this model, the students are located in the same place (eg Malaysia), but that will not be the same place as the degree-awarding institution (eg Australia). This has the benefit of the student being able to stay at home (or at least nearer to home) to receive their international education. The students are taught by teachers who are local to them, rather than staff from the degree-awarding institution (although some may give 'guest lectures'). There is likely to be a link person from the degree-awarding institution who oversees quality assurance and quality enhancement with the local provider through regular visits to the partner.

In some of these models, eg twinning arrangements and articulation, there is expectation that the students will move for part of their education. In an articulation agreement, students might complete a certain number of credits with the local provider and then gain direct access further into a programme at the degree-awarding institution. These arrangements are often termed 2+2, 3+1 or 2+1, depending on the ratio of study in each location. In joint, dual and multiple degrees, the emphasis is on collaboration, with *'mutual recognition of systems and academic input'* (Doorbar and Bateman, 2008, p 18). This can result in degrees from more than one institution, or in a collaborative award. There might be opportunities for students to study in the different collaborating institutions; through the University of Glasgow-Nankai University Joint Graduate School, for example, students are able to study both in Tianjin (China) and Glasgow (Scotland) as part of two-year masters' programmes in Environmental Science, International Relations, Translation Studies and Urban and Regional Planning, which results in dual masters' qualifications from the University of Glasgow and Nankai University.

Physical presence models

Associated terms: international branch campus, joint university, international study centre, flying faculty

The most visible approach to TNE is through the international branch campus (IBC), which is *'an international campus, wholly or partly owned, by the degree-awarding institution, which delivers its own degrees'* (Healey, 2013, p 9) or *'a satellite operation of a parent HEI'* (Knight and McNamara, 2017, p 15). The IBC will have a physical presence in the host country with buildings and branding that connect it with the degree-awarding institution, and staff who are either permanently based in or seconded there. Students will, usually, come from the region where the IBC is located. IBCs are not all the same and what is or is not defined as an IBC can and does change (Lane and Kinser, 2012) making comparison between them difficult. IBCs are what Lane and Kinser (2012) describe as one of the various types of foreign outposts operated by colleges and universities. Others would include the joint university, where both providing and host countries are involved in the development and operation of the university and the international study centre, which provides a presence in the overseas location, but is not a full IBC.

Finally, flying faculty approaches provide the physical presence of degree-awarding institution staff in the host country, although there is not the permanent physical presence in the country that is apparent with the IBC. Here, degree-awarding institution staff members fly in and teach for short periods and then fly out again (K Smith, 2009, p 111). The students are based in the host country and receive instruction from degree-awarding institution teachers at various points in their programmes. In between visits, they might be supported by local tutors, or remain in contact with the flying faculty teachers through virtual learning environments.

Critical issues

TNE as a neo-colonial project

One major criticism of TNE delivery models is that they continue a modern form of colonialism, where the former colonisers dominate those in the developing world, bringing their own worldviews and language and thus maintaining Western superiority. The following examples focus on IBCs but are relevant to other TNE approaches.

Siltaoja et al (2019) use a neo-colonial frame to explore 'world-class' discourse in business schools. They found that IBCs (located in the United Arab Emirates (UAE)) reproduce a 'fantasy' of world-class ideals, particularly through their marketing materials. This positions IBCs as something superior and inherently (and unproblematically) Western. Interviews with IBC staff explored how they complied with or resisted this construct of world-classness through three types of mimicry (cynical, bounded and failed). They conclude that in IBCs there is a desire to both replicate and resist Western practices and that tensions arise through the clash of global

→

and local norms. The winner, they argue, is always the world-class fantasy that everyone seeks to protect.

The Vice Chancellor of Heriot Watt University, located in Scotland, Malaysia and Dubai, challenges such a *'colonial UK base camp outlook'*. Williams (2018) states that his university does not have branch campuses, but operates as a single university, with an integrated quality assurance and enhancement framework, and identical degrees, which enable students to be truly mobile across the three locations. For Williams, the model is not one of neo-colonialism, but of authentic collaborative development.

What I have tried to do here is provide an overview of the predominant models of TNE, and the provision they encompass. Although I have situated these approaches within three models, the boundaries between them are often not that clear-cut. Knight's (2016) classification of independent and collaborative TNE adds another dimension to the classification of delivery models. Knight (2016, p 38) notes that TNE can be delivered independently (eg no local provider is involved in the design or delivery of the programmes) or collaboratively (eg cooperation with a local partner to deliver the programme). These nuances mean that there are many permutations of TNE provision; for instance, an institution could offer dual degrees, validations and have franchised provision with the same overseas partner.

Critical questions for practice

» Can you identify the different TNE models being used within your institution and across different departments and programmes?

» Which models do you prefer and why?

» How have your own experiences shaped your view of what TNE is?

How has TNE developed, where are we currently at and where are we heading?

I started this chapter by noting that higher education has always been mobile – but what has happened more recently is a shift in the form of mobility. While there has always been the movement of staff and students across borders (Medieval European universities, for example, were very international), the movement of higher education programmes and institutions is a relatively new occurrence (Stella, 2006), although the University of London provides early and enduring examples of TNE. Since 1858, its London International Programme has opened up study to all those who meet the programme's entry requirements and can pay the fee (O'Callaghan, 2017).

Knight and Liu (2016, p 1) chart the evolution of higher education's movement across borders, which I have represented diagrammatically in Figure 1.1.

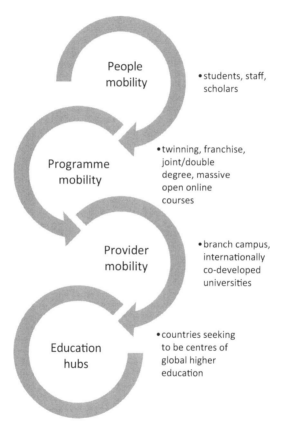

Figure 1.1 The evolution of higher education cross-border mobility.

The evolution has seen a shift from the movement of people to the movement of programmes and providers. More recent developments have seen countries establishing themselves as education hubs, in recognition of their desire to be a regional centre of excellence for research and education. Countries positioning them-selves as education hubs include Qatar, UAE, Singapore, Malaysia, Hong Kong and Botswana (Knight and Liu, 2016).

Example 1.1

Education hubs

Education hubs are established in countries that want to position themselves within the region as a centre for higher education and research. Education hubs are a national-level transnational strategy that require substantial investment from the host country (Knight, 2015). The Incheon Global Campus (IGC) in South Korea, for example, has received 918 million USD of investment from central and local government. The IGC has positioned itself as the leader of global education in North East Asia, seeking to attract 10,000 students to study at one of the ten universities which will be situated there. See Jo (2017).

This evolution has been relatively quick and the increasing focus on TNE (programme and provider mobility) reflects *the boom in the international trade in education'* (Naidoo, 2009, p 310). Higher education is a valuable commodity for both importing and exporting countries and while some would reject this commodification of higher education, it has certainly contributed to its growth.

The scale and scope of trade in TNE

While it is recognised that globally TNE is growing, it is hard to find accurate data about the scale and scope of TNE. There are some global trends reported; for example, the majority of degree programmes offered through TNE are at master's level, the most popular subjects are business, management and engineering (British Council, 2012a), and most courses are taught in English. While there is fluctuation in the TNE market, the USA, Australia and UK along with New Zealand and Canada have been key exporters of education for some time (Naidoo, 2009). Importers of higher education have tended to be situated in the Far East (eg Hong Kong, Singapore, China and Malaysia) and the Gulf States (eg Oman, Qatar and Dubai) and some of these importer countries have positioned themselves as education hubs. Increasingly the divide between importer and exporter countries is blurring. Traditionally, China has imported higher education but now also engages in its export; eg Peking University has opened an IBC in the UK (Pells, 2019).

It is also difficult to make cross-country comparisons because many countries do not collect robust data on TNE (Knight and McNamara, 2017). The UK, however, has a well-developed data collection plan for TNE activity; the UK provides an example of TNE at a national level.

Example 1.2

TNE in the UK

UK universities currently provide qualifications to more students who are based overseas than they do to international students studying in the UK. In 2015–2016, there were just over 700,000 UK TNHE students (UUKi, 2018). UK TNHE was worth £610 million in 2016, increasing by 72 per cent between 2010–2016 (DIT, 2019). In 2015–16, 82% of UK universities were engaged in TNE, and 23 universities had 5000 or more TNE students (UUKi, 2018). Collaborative provision has always been prominent in UK TNE and it accounted for 44 per cent of provision in 2015–2016 (UUKi, 2018). Malaysia and Singapore hosted the most TNE students, and UK IBCs are most prevalent in Asia and the Middle East (UUKi, 2018). In 2012–2013, the most popular TNE subject area was business and management, accounting for 46 per cent of enrolments (BIS, 2014). Sixty-five per cent of TNE students are undergraduate (UUKi, 2018). The data from 2016–2017 shows a slowdown in the growth of UK TNE; this reflects a maturation of higher education systems of some of the host countries the UK operates in, and a movement away from lighter-touch TNE models (such as franchising and validation) towards models that require more institutional commitment (Inge, 2018).

As TNE matures, there are likely to be changes in the power and relationships between partners, resulting in more equitable partnerships and collaborative TNE delivery models (Knight, 2017).

Chapter outlines

The rest of this book looks more closely at the practice of transnational higher education. Chapter 2 focuses on motivations for engagement in TNE at national, institutional and practitioner levels; Chapter 3 looks at the quality assurance of TNE; Chapter 4 profiles TNE students and considers their experiences; and Chapter 5 looks at the work of those engaged in TNE. In Chapter 6, the book ends with reflections on the inspiration for this book, the journey it has taken us on, and some thoughts on the future of TNE.

Summary

- TNE is one aspect of the internationalisation agenda and refers to the movement of programmes and institutions across national borders to where the students are located.

- Offshore, cross-border and borderless education are all terms that are used instead of, or interchangeably with TNE.

- TNE can encompass many things from distance learning through to IBCs and there is a plethora of overlapping terminology.

- TNE is constantly evolving – entering new markets, applying new models and developing new ways of working.

Useful texts

Knight, J (2015) Transnational Education Remodeled: Toward a Common TNE Framework and Definitions, *Journal of Studies in International Education*, 20: 34–47.

Anything by Jane Knight about internationalisation, cross-border or transnational education will be useful. In this article, Knight discusses some of the difficulties of definition and calls for a common framework of categories and definitions to describe TNE.

UUKi (2018) *The Scale of UK Higher Education Transnational Education 2015– 2016 – Trend Analysis of HESA Data.* London: UUK. [online] Available at: www.universitiesuk.ac.uk/policy-and-analysis/reports/Pages/the-scale-of-UK-higher-education-transnational-education-2015–16.aspx (accessed 14 March 2020).

Reports on national trends, when they are available, provide interesting data on TNE. This report from Universities UK International presents Higher Education Statistics Agency (HESA) Aggregate Overseas Record (AOR) data from 2015–2016.

Who is motivated to engage in TNE?

Chapter 1 outlined what TNE encompasses, different delivery models of TNE, and the different roles that nations play in TNE as exporter countries (eg where the degree-awarding institution is situated, sometimes called 'home' countries) and importer countries (sometimes called 'host' countries). In this chapter, the motivations for engaging in TNE are explored in more detail. It will probably come as no surprise that the motivations for engagement in TNE are just as complex as the very definitions of TNE themselves, and will vary according to the practitioners involved, the institutions they work in, the countries in which they are situated and the global environment in which they operate. I have found a stacked Venn diagram useful (Figure 2.1) to show how motivations are interrelated and embedded one within another.

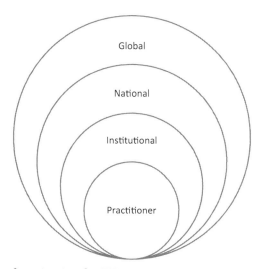

Figure 2.1 Levels of motivation for TNE.

At each of the levels above, there will be different drivers for engaging in TNE; but these themselves are not static; they are dynamic, overlapping and complicated. TNE is ever-evolving, and as TNE develops, as the relationships between the TNE partners mature, and as national priorities change, so too will the motivations for engagement. It is not possible to outline all of the potential motivations for the multitude of partner relationships that TNE supports within the scope of this book; however, what I aim to do is to outline some of the key drivers, at each of the levels above, to consider in relation to your own practice and context. The following question is explored.

» What are some of the drivers for engagement in TNE globally, nationally, institutionally and for practitioners?

Global

As discussed within Chapter 1, TNE is a feature of a strong drive within higher education towards internationalisation. At a global level, the economic, political, cultural and technological drivers for internationalisation have framed its development (McBurnie and Ziguras, 2007). The rise of TNE globally is often contextualised in light of the General Agreement on Trade in Services (GATS), which favours free trade and the increase in private higher education provision to meet the needs of the growing demand for higher education, particularly in developing countries (Kosmützky and Putty, 2016; Marginson and van der Wende, 2007).

GATS, a World Trade Organisation (WTO) agreement with a focus on services, came into being following the Uruguay Rounds in 1995. It was inspired by the same aims as its trade counterpart, the General Agreement on Tariffs and Trade (GATT); those aims are:

Creating a credible and reliable system of international trade rules; ensuring fair and equitable treatment of all participants (principle of non-discrimination); stimulating economic activity through guaranteed policy bindings; and promoting trade and development through progressive liberalization.

(WTO, n d)

Higher education is viewed as a tradeable service, which operates according to four 'modes of supply'. How these modes relate to TNE are summarised and tabulated in Table 2.1 (drawn from Hou et al, 2014, p 302; McBurnie and Ziguras, 2007, pp 138–41; WTO, nd; Ziguras and McBurnie, 2008, pp 9–10). The examples are given according to Mode, but it should be recognised that most TNE will involve the operation of more than one Mode simultaneously (McBurnie and Ziguras, 2007, p 139).

Table 2.1 GATS modes of supply and examples from TNE (WTO definitions from WTO (nd).

Mode	WTO definition	TNE example
Cross-border supply	Services flow from the territory of one Member into the territory of another Member (eg banking or architectural services transmitted via telecommunications or mail).	An online course provided by a South African university to students in Zimbabwe.
Consumption abroad	Situations where a service consumer (eg tourist or patient) moves into another Member's territory to obtain a service.	A Chinese student engaging in part or the whole of their degree in the USA.
Commercial presence	A service supplier of one Member establishes a territorial presence, including through ownership or lease of premises, in another Member's territory to provide a service (eg domestic subsidiaries of foreign insurance companies or hotel chains).	An Australian university establishing an IBC in Malaysia.
Presence of natural persons	Persons of one Member entering the territory of another Member to supply a service (eg accountants, doctors or teachers).	Lecturers from the UK travelling to teach in Egypt for short, intensive blocks.

TNE, in an era of trade liberalisation, is deemed to bring the following benefits: access to foreign markets for more competitive domestic markets; consumer access to services from foreign suppliers; and more predictable trade systems (Hart, 2002, p 5, cited in McBurnie and Ziguras, 2007, p 143). TNE can generate income for those economies with developed higher education systems, where they can meet domestic demand and where state funding has failed to meet the needs of higher education institutions (Wilkins and Huisman, 2012). Equally, the freeing up of the system can be beneficial for importing economies who have greater demand for higher education, due to economic and political reasons, than the domestic market can meet. The motivations for nations will be discussed further below.

The trade liberalisation of higher education has received criticism, mostly in relation to the perceived lack of governmental control over the regulation of higher education when faced with incoming private providers; a shift in the principal role of higher education away from a public good to a tradeable service; the homogenisation of global higher education; and the threat of cultural imperialism.

Critical issues

TNE and cultural imperialism

As already discussed, TNE is sometimes perceived as a neo-colonial project. Equally, critics have associated TNE with cultural or educational imperialism through the transmission of what is usually Western curricula from a degree-awarding institution, usually situated within a developed country, to students in a less developed country using the English medium, on the understanding that the students will adapt because 'the West is Best'. This transmission model is premised on the view of the educational exporters as aggressive colonisers, and educational importers as the passive colonised. While there are often power differentials in TNE (as we will see later), this view is rather simplistic (Phan, 2017, p 3). As McBurnie and Ziguras (2007, p 71) argue, receiving cultures are not so fragile that overexposure to the West will cause them to '*burn up and blow away like ash in the wind*' nor are they unwilling recipients or passive recipients of TNE; instead they play their own part in '*creating and sustaining a desire for "Western education" and "Western knowledge"*' (Phan, 2017, p 31) and wield their own power, based on their own interests and for their own gain, in the providers and programmes they welcome.

While there are global imperatives for TNE, individual nations have their own motivations for engagement.

National

In this section, three key national drivers for engagement in TNE are explored: TNE as export revenue; TNE as capacity development for national higher education systems; and TNE as a provider of societal benefits.

Export revenues

The increasing commercialisation of higher education has led, as indicated above, to countries with excess capacity providing education to students in countries where there is a limited supply (McBurnie and Ziguras, 2007, p 1). As a tradeable service, TNE has economic value and can prove an important source of income for major exporting countries (such as Australia, the UK, USA and New Zealand).

Example 2.1

Exporting (TNE) is 'GREAT'

In 2017, the Department for International Trade (DIT) in the UK announced an initiative to help the education sector operate in overseas markets (DIT, 2017), as part of its *Exporting is GREAT* programme (DIT, 2015). The aim of the initiative was to '*help the sector unlock its commercial potential and meet the huge demand for British education around the world*' (DIT, 2017). Speaking of the venture, the then Minister for Investment, Mark Garnier, said:

The UK is already a world-leader in education exports and this sector will be vital for our future trading relationships. We know the demand is there, and I want to see even more UK education providers exporting their expertise.

(DIT, 2017)

A DIT Education Advisory Group was established to provide a forum for senior leaders in the education sector to explore global trade and investment opportunities and discuss how the government could support the UK education sector overseas.

In 2016, UK revenue from education exports and TNE was estimated to be £19.9 billion, of which £1.9 billion is revenue from TNE, £610 million from transnational higher education specifically, and £30 million from further education, £110 million from English language training, and £1.1 billion from schools. The revenue from transnational higher education has increased by 72 per cent since 2010 (DIT, 2019).

It is not only those countries that have traditionally been exporting higher education that seek to generate export income through TNE; many importing countries are also trying to become net exporters of higher education through the development of education hubs and niche education exports (McBurnie and Ziguras, 2007, p 4).

Example 2.2

Malaysia's ambitions in the export of education

In Malaysia, the National Strategic Plan of 2007 outlined plans for Malaysia to become a major exporter of higher education by 2020; part of its strategy is to become a regional hub for higher education and the country has invited reputable international universities to set up branch campuses and offer niche programmes. A key driver for this approach is to bring international students to Malaysia and benefit from their fees and in-country spending, and to reduce loss of income to the country if Malaysian students pursue their education overseas (Ahmad and Buchanan, 2016, pp 165–6).

Not all motivations for engagement in TNE, however, have such a strong financial impetus.

Meeting unmet demand for higher education

In some countries, the demand for higher education far outstrips the supply. Growing middle classes combined with insufficient, or restricted, public universities systems mean that some countries cannot meet the needs and desires of their own potential student population. While some students might have access to higher education overseas, prohibitive costs, inconvenience and the potential of brain drain have motivated nations to engage in TNE in order to grow their provision of higher education, as Example 2.3 below shows.

Example 2.3

Provision for non-nationals in UAE

In 2014, only 1.4 million of the 9.2 million people in the UAE were Emirati citizens. The remaining 7.8 million non-national residents were not eligible for the benefits of citizenship, such as free education in public universities. As a result, the three federal universities in the UAE, which account for 30 per cent of student enrolment, are populated with 90 per cent Emirati citizens. Private universities, which include IBCs, cater for the expatriate, non-national population and international students coming to the UAE for study (QAA, 2017).

National capacity development

Capacity development is defined here as an approach to development that improves a *'nation's ability to provide for itself'* (McBurnie and Ziguras, 2007, p 80). Capacity development can take the form of the specific skills that students can gain from their TNE studies that then result in a more skilled workforce and the subsequent sharing of those skills with others within the nation as professionals or educators (Mellors-Bourne, 2017).

Capacity development does not only relate to workplace skills but can also be in the area of educational capability. China is currently engaging in TNE to support the modernisation and improvement of *'teaching practices, quality assurance standards, programme and curriculum development, and academic management and governance matters'* (British Council, 2013, p 8). The motivation for Chinese engagement in TNE is what Healey (2015, p 8) calls *'capacity absorbing'*, that is, complementing, and through competition, enhancing Chinese higher education. Engagement in TNE can facilitate the development of local higher education systems.

A further motivation for engagement in TNE is the creation of knowledge through research collaboration, the cross-fertilisation of ideas and capacity development for researchers. Collaborative research partnerships are often one of the least developed aspects of TNE and might require the maturation of relationships before fruition.

Growing capacity for higher education and capacity development more generally can lead to broader societal benefits (Mellors-Bourne, 2017, p 10).

Societal benefit

A key motivator among some nations for engagement in TNE is that it brings societal benefit. In order to achieve these benefits, a driver for TNE is the expansion of access to higher education in less developed countries and remote and rural areas (Mitchell, 2018). The benefits are realised through an expanded educated and skilled workforce that can serve the national interest.

In China, for example, the view of TNE is that it should support *'public interest'* (Hou et al, 2014, p 308). There is a strong demand for higher education in China and currently a limited supply due to the relatively small number of Chinese universities. TNE provides a means to widen access through partnerships with foreign higher education providers. This ambition may not, however, always reach those in most need, as outlined in the following Critical issue.

Critical issues

Meeting societal aims through TNE

China aims to widen access to higher education through its Sino-foreign partnerships; although the will is there, in reality, as Hou et al (2014) show, the most socially and economically deprived areas of China are still not benefitting from TNE, as TNE programmes are mostly situated in the more developed eastern coastal regions. Remote and less economically developed provinces are less effective in attracting TNE providers; the cost of TNE means that wealthier areas are more attractive to providers; and TNE fees can be prohibitive for students from deprived families (Hou et al, 2014). Indeed, Tsang (2013) argues that TNE provides a means for the new Chinese middle classes to reproduce their advantaged class status. Middle-class parents, whose children do not achieve well in the *gaokao* (the highly competitive national university entrance exam) and cannot access the best Chinese universities, are eschewing lower-ranking local universities and using their social and political capital to secure entry into private universities, including those engaging in TNE with the aim of subsequently sending their children to study overseas. Tsang (2013) suggests this approach consolidates the new Chinese middle classes and supports intergenerational upward mobility.

Malaysia has similar widening access ambitions (Hill et al, 2014). Like China there was excess demand for higher education that the public universities were unable to meet. Private providers were encouraged to fill this gap. These private providers did not have degree-awarding powers and so partnered with foreign universities. Such TNE partnerships were promoted and supported by the Malaysian government. The expansion of access worked, with a 131 per cent increase in private institution enrolment between 2000 and 2010 (Hill et al, 2014, p 961).

Finally, nations that export higher education might also see their contribution to TNE as a contribution to local development agendas and capacity building (Mitchell, 2018), or as a form of altruistic *'intellectual aid'* (Hoare, 2012). As Illevia (cited in Mitchell, 2018) argues, such engagement should be attractive to developed countries, with aid programmes that support teaching partnerships for capacity building at home. The results can be mutually beneficial and enriching and can bring reputational benefits to the exporting partner.

Critical questions for practice

» Within your own country, what do you see as the national drivers for engagement in TNE?

» How is TNE promoted by your national government?

Institutional

Many types of institutions engage in TNE, for example public or private universities; institutions that have foundation, taught or research degree awarding powers (QAA, 2018b, p 3); private for-profit and not-for profit organisations and entrepreneurs (see Fielden, 2013, p 13). The key motivators for TNE for institutions will be discussed, focusing specifically on income generation, strategic alliances, international profile and reputation, and capacity development.

Income generation

Many TNE partner institutions are privately funded and rely on revenue from TNE to survive (Kemp, 2018); for publicly funded institutions, TNE engagement might enable the introduction of attractive subject areas and programmes that are not currently offered. The idea of income generation can be equally attractive for the degree-awarding institutions. As shown in the UK *Exporting (TNE) is 'GREAT'* example, the export potential of education has been promoted by governments, positioning education as a valuable and tradeable national asset. It is true that TNE can enable institutions to enter new markets and extend reach to greater numbers of students, thereby providing a potentially rich income stream. In terms of TNE models, distance learning offers the strongest opportunities for income generation (Mellors-Bourne et al, 2014, p 10). Indirect revenue can also be gained when students, who having participated in a TNE programme, choose to continue their education at the degree-awarding institution. A further potential revenue stream, for the exporting institution, is through the philanthropic donations from foreign alumni to their *alma mater*; this form of income, however, is still relatively under-developed, in the UK at least (Mellors-Bourne, 2017, p 76).

TNE does not, however, always bring income. There are many examples where there is little financial gain from TNE, and, indeed, cases where TNE engagement had grave financial implications.

Example 2.4

The financial drain of an IBC

IBCs are particularly risky financial commitments that can be a significant financial drain on the home campus. In 2019, the *Times Higher Education* (*THE*) reported on the University of Reading's (UK) experience with its campus in Malaysia (Bothwell, 2019). Opened in 2016, the IBC reported a loss of £27 milliion in 2017–2018 and led to a £20 million deficit for the University of Reading as a whole. The university, which has already invested £21 million in the IBC, needs to invest at least a further £40–45 million over the next five years to support the campus. *THE* noted that the reasons for the significant shortfall include: the IBC's location in a less popular area of Malaysia, which hampered recruitment; difficulties with visa and accreditation procedures; and a later and more costly opening than originally planned. A source told the *THE* that '*it is a salutary lesson. You can't make a quick buck opening overseas campuses*' (Bothwell, 2019).

In some cases, the aim, rather than income generation, is financial sustainability, with institutions preferring to focus on other drivers, such as strategic alliances, reputational gains and capacity development.

Strategic alliances

The development of strategic alliances with other providers is another institutional motivation for engagement in TNE. For importing institutions, alliances might support the development of niche programmes in subject areas that they currently lack the capacity to offer (eg the franchise agreement between St George's, University of London and the University of Nicosia to bring the first medical programmes to Cyprus [WECD/UUKi, 2018, pp 42–3]) or, for both partners, opportunities to engage in collaborations to support knowledge production (eg the partnership between Central Luzon State University and Bicol University in the Philippines and the University of Liverpool in the UK to develop research and postgraduate training programmes around sustainable food systems [WECD/UUKi, 2018, pp 30–31]).

A TNE partnership can offer opportunities for importing institutions to gain international accreditation for programmes that would not be possible without a TNE partnership, and for some institutions without degree-awarding powers, the TNE partnership is the only way they can offer degrees (Hill et al, 2014).

International profile and reputation

The formation of strategic alliances with universities that can enhance an institution's international profile is a strong motivator for some institutions. In her work exploring elite strategic alliances with Chinese universities, Montgomery (2016, p 76) found that *'Chinese universities seek TNHE partnerships with high-ranking universities across the globe'*, thus further extending their international reach and reputation.

We are operating in an increasingly competitive global higher education market and developing a 'global brand' is important. For some institutions, this might mean developing an institutional strategy for internationalisation that includes TNE, or emphasising global reach in mission statements, visions and marketing. The UK's De Montfort University (DMU) *Strategic Plan (2018–2023)*, for example, sets out its vision for TNE through the building of global partnerships:

Build global partnerships based on a shared ethos in order to raise our international profile, with a target of increasing our income from transnational education activities by £5 million, and realise an ambition to open a new overseas base.

(DMU, nd, p 12)

The perceived 'brand globalness' (ie the perception consumers hold of the brand being global) (Akram et al, 2011, p 293) is not solely defined by overseas presence or strategic direction. In their work on perceptions of IBCs, Chee et al (2016) found that for universities from developed countries, students saw home and IBCs as similar (in terms of reputation, quality and brand equity), whereas for universities from developing countries, there was a perception among students that the home campus was better. This means that it can be difficult for universities from developing countries to expand internationally (Chee et al, 2016, p 97). For the importing institution, however, partnering with an OECD member can help improve local public perception of their own institution and can go some way to developing their reputation within their own countries (McBurnie and Ziguras, 2007).

TNE shapes and is shaped by reputation. Engagement in TNE can greatly enhance reputation, and reputation can enhance engagement in TNE. Equally, however, engagement in TNE can pose a significant reputational risk, as will be explored further in Chapter 3.

Institutional capacity development

A final institutional motivator is capacity development. There has often been a portrayal of TNE as being a means of *'bringing the best from the West to a developing country'* (Bodycott and Walker, 2000, p 81), which has fuelled the debates about imperialism or neo-colonialism outlined earlier. Yet this is not always as one-sided as such a portrayal suggests. Hou et al (2014, p 214) have noted that Chinese universities actively engage in TNE in order to *absorb high quality education resources* into their own system, thus fostering learning and teaching innovation, and Sutrisno and Pillay (2013, p 1192) reported that an Indonesian university was able to learn from their partner's *curriculum material, teaching design, and delivery methodology'.* Equally, for those who export education, engagement in TNE can foster internationalisation at home as practitioners bring their TNE experiences into their home-campus classrooms.

Access to transnational research collaborations is another driver for engagement in TNE. Initial TNE relations might develop into research collaborations (Sutrisno and Pillay, 2013), which can be mutually beneficial in terms of access to expertise, different research populations and contexts, and alternative sources of funding, which will all contribute to capacity development for transnational and globally relevant research, which are often well received in research assessment exercises.

Finally, transnational staff exchange, for research and teaching, can support institutional capacity development by exposing those staff to different ways of working in cultures and contexts that might be less familiar and this can be particularly beneficial for practitioners involved.

Critical questions for practice

» What do you perceive to be the main drivers for engagement in TNE within your institution?

» What motivates your institution's partners to engage?

» Are these motivations aligned?

Practitioners

TNE is operationalised by practitioners and they bring with them their own motivations for engaging transnationally. Clearly, for some staff there is less motivation and more expectation that TNE is part of, or an extension of, their formal academic role (eg Dass, 2019, p 177). Other staff, however, might actively choose to engage.

In my own work looking at flying faculty teachers' motivations, challenges and opportunities (Smith, 2014), the following drivers were reported.

» The opportunity to visit new places, gain different perspectives, expand worldviews.

» Engagement with new ideas and perspectives, freshen teaching practices at home and overseas.

» Meet new people, sustain relationships and develop friendships.

» Enhance own personal profile within own institution and seek promotion.

» Develop research and consultancy links.

These motivations were expressed by flying faculty staff, who visited the importing country to teach. Yet, similar motivations exist for others engaged in TNE, both within the degree-awarding and the host institution. Another key driver might be finances. Engagement in TNE sometimes results in supplementary payments; low academic salaries in the host country may encourage academics to work as local tutors across multiple sites and TNE programmes to boost income (Dass, 2019, p 184). Further motivations include the chance to work with former colleagues, a previous institution or with an *alma mater*.

Example 2.5

Non-Chinese staff at an IBC in China

In an interview study with non-Chinese staff working at an IBC in China, Cai and Hall (2016) identified similar motivations. Their respondents talked of seeking adventure and a change of lifestyle. China was a pull, in terms of the food, culture, language and family connections. For some, work in China was described as an investment in their children's future and provided career-enhancing possibilities through leadership opportunities, promotion, increased research productivity and growing professional networks. For younger academics, the IBC posting was financially lucrative, and for more experienced practitioners, it offered a means to contribute to the development of the campus through the sharing of that experience.

Engagement in TNE can provide opportunities for ongoing professional development and access to further professional courses (eg accredited programmes to support lecturer development), which can motivate some. Within my work, I have been a strong proponent of TNE as a means to stimulate personal and professional learning and development (Smith, 2009, 2013) that, with support, could prove to be a significant motivator for individuals.

Critical question for practice

» What is driving you to engage in TNE?

Summary

- There are many varied motivations for engaging in TNE.

- Motivations depend on the practitioners involved, the institutions they work in, the countries they are situated in and the prevailing global environment.

- Motivations overlap, interact and change over time depending on the partners involved.

Useful texts

McBurnie, G and Ziguras, C (2007) *Transnational Education: Issues and Trends in Offshore Higher Education*. Abingdon: Routledge.

Although written over a decade ago, this book provides a comprehensive overview of TNE, including discussions on motivations for engagement.

Phan, L H (2017) *Transnational Education Crossing 'Asia' and 'the West': Adjusted Desire, Transformative Mediocrity, Neo-Colonial Desire*. London: Routledge.

A more recent book, by Phan Le-Ha, problematises TNE from a non-Western perspective and challenges us to think differently and critically about the complexities of engagement in TNE.

Why are questions of quality key in TNE?

Chapter 2 outlined some of the benefits of engaging in TNE and the global, national, institutional and practitioner motivations for that engagement. Decisions to engage in TNE are not, however, taken lightly because TNE carries the potential for reputational risk when things do not work out. The perception of TNE has been tarnished by poor-quality education from inexperienced and irreputable providers. In unregulated settings, fraudulent practices such as '"*diploma mills", rogue providers, fake accreditation agencies, fly-by-night academics or grade inflation*' (Nahn and Nguyen, 2018, p 141) taint TNE. But even in regulated TNE, there is a general mistrust (Stella, 2006) and an underlying perception that TNE is just not as good as the education offered at home campuses, that TNE is '*mediocre*', and that the '*increasing demand from average-level students has made low- to average-quality transnational education possible and sustainable*' (Phan, 2017, p 221). These perceptions are clearly unhelpful not only for TNE students and institutions, but also for national higher education systems. Students should be able to expect a high-quality TNE experience; poor-quality TNE can be financially and reputationally damaging for institutions. Individual institutions and national higher education systems' reputations rest on the quality of their academic awards, and that is why quality assurance processes feature so prominently in practitioners' daily experiences of TNE (L Smith, 2009, p 470).

Those nations and providers who want to maintain their standing and reputations in relation to TNE now place increased emphasis on questions of quality, and how quality can be assured and improved when operating across more than one educational system. Just like the motivations for TNE, quality assurance is operationalised globally, nationally, institutionally and by practitioners. This chapter seeks to problematise quality procedures around key themes of standardisation, convergence, equivalence and collaboration, and will focus on the following questions.

» What is quality assurance in higher education and in TNE more specifically?

» How are academic standards assured in TNE?

» How are approaches to quality assurance in TNE standardising and harmonising higher education?

» What does collaboration in quality assurance look like in TNE?

Quality assurance of TNE

The quality of educational experiences is important for the reputation of TNE. In relation to quality assurance, McBurnie and Ziguras (2007, p 107) note that there is less resistance to the quality assurance of TNE than there is within domestic programmes. The acceptance of the need for quality assurance stems from the different contexts in which the education is delivered, the different staff involved, the different responsibilities of the partners, and the requirements of home and host country regulations.

But what is quality and what is quality assurance in higher education? Just like TNE, the concept of quality is difficult to define; it is multifaceted, context-specific and historically situated. In their seminal work on defining quality, Harvey and Green (1993) view quality as:

- » exceptional (ie distinctive; excellent; meeting threshold standards);
- » perfection or consistency (ie no defects; getting things right the first time);
- » fitness for purpose (ie whether the product/service meets its purpose; the fulfilment of an institution's mission);
- » value for money (ie efficiency and effectiveness; accountability; performance indicators; student charters);
- » transformative (ie a qualitative change; enhancement; student empowerment).

Of these different definitions (and the others that followed, eg Schindler et al, 2015), 'fitness for purpose' is the one most widely accepted in education (McBurnie and Ziguras, 2007; Woodhouse, 1999). Quality as fitness for purpose allows institutions to define their own mission and values, enabling variability between higher education providers (Woodhouse, 1999, p 29). Quality assurance refers to the *'policies, attitudes, actions and procedures necessary to ensure that quality is being maintained and enhanced'* (Woodhouse, 1999, p 30). While quality assurance procedures are enacted institutionally, these are often monitored by external quality review agencies through audits, assessments, accreditation, recognition, evaluations and reviews. The aim of external quality review is to hold higher education institutions to account for the resources they receive, make an independent judgment of quality and support institutions to improve (Woodhouse, 1999, p 30).

Quality assurance is challenging transnationally, as it involves different contexts and different cultures, which are often geographically distant. As shown in Chapter 1, there are many different models of TNE, which operate differently and may not fit smoothly into existing quality assurance processes (Choudaha and Edelstein, 2014). The global mobility of graduates means there is a need for qualifications to be recognised across borders (Stella, 2006). There can be tensions between the academic and commercial priorities, which result in different understandings of what quality is, and how quality should be assured.

In their review of literature relating to TNE, Kosmützky and Putty (2015, p 18) outline the further complexities of quality assurance in TNE:

» the dual roles that countries play if they are both exporters and importers of higher education;

» the different rationales for regulation and the meaning and significance of quality assurance across different countries;

» less well-developed national frameworks for quality assurance in many countries, which may not be compatible with the requirements of international accreditation.

The drivers to establish robust quality assurance systems are strong, and they can be seen at different levels: globally, nationally and institutionally.

The operationalisation of quality assurance in TNE

International frameworks and convergence in quality assurance

While there are many frameworks to assure quality across the world, there is a perception that these frameworks are becoming more similar. This is due, according to McBurnie and Ziguras (2007, p 121), to a general agreement on the principles that should govern TNE between importing and exporting governments, professional bodies and international agencies. This mirrors other convergence movements in higher education such as the diffusion of educational approaches and ideas (eg blended learning and graduate attributes), appropriation of educational policies across regions, the spread of national qualification frameworks, the increased use of rankings and metrics, and the alignment of university mission statements, visions and strategies, which all contribute to the harmonisation of standards, expectations and experiences of higher education. Although this drive to convergence is strong, there is a danger of homogeneity and isomorphism, where diversity and experimentation are reduced. The risks of standardisation in relation to TNE are discussed later in this chapter.

While there might now be increasing convergence in terms of approaches to the quality assurance of TNE, when UNESCO and the OECD set about developing the *Guidelines for Quality Provision in Cross-Border Higher Education* (OECD, 2005) in 2004, some national agencies were not able to deal with the challenges of TNE provision. Although there has been an increase in quality assurance and accrediting bodies, *'existing national quality assurance capacity often focuses exclusively on domestic delivery by domestic institutions'* (Vincent-Lancrin and Pfotenhauer 2012, p 10). A key aim in terms of the development of the *Guidelines* was in establishing international collaboration and networking, transparent sharing of information and systems for quality assurance, and a commitment to capacity building (Vincent-Lancrin and Pfotenhauer, 2012, p 10). The *Guidelines* are written as a set of recommendations for six TNE stakeholder groups: governments; higher education institutions/providers including academic staff; student bodies; quality assurance and accreditation bodies; academic recognition bodies; and professional bodies (OECD, 2005). A survey administered in 2010 suggested that there was a high level of compliance with the *Guidelines* among the identified stakeholders, particularly governments, higher education institutions and quality assurance and accreditation bodies (Vincent-Lancrin and Pfotenhauer, 2012, p 5). Blackmur (2007) provides a strong critique of the *Guidelines*, where he challenges the very rationale on which they were developed, and questions whether the most appropriate instruments (here quality assurance and accreditation systems) were chosen to maximise the net benefits of the internationalisation of higher education.

Critical questions for practice

» Does your institution, and do you, meet the recommendations outlined in the OECD *Guidelines*?

» Do you feel you should?

The *Guidelines* are voluntary; there is no shared international framework for the quality assurance of TNE. When it comes to the operationalisation of quality assurance, codes of conduct and frameworks from national agencies guide what happens in relation to quality within institutions. Quality assurance of TNE comes under the scrutiny of different stakeholders, including the degree-awarding institution, the partner institution, quality assurance agencies of the exporting country, the quality assurance agencies in the importing country, and any professional bodies. In this section, I focus on guidance provided by national agencies and how that is operationalised institutionally.

National approaches

Many countries have national agencies that are tasked to safeguard the quality and standards of higher education.

Below are some examples from key exporters and importers of TNE.

> » **AQA** – Academic Quality Agency for New Zealand universities – New Zealand;
>
> » **HKCAAVQ** – Hong Kong Council for Accreditation of Academic and Vocational Qualifications – Hong Kong;
>
> » **UQAIB** – University and Quality Assurance International Board (private providers in free zones) and **CAA** – Commission for Academic Accreditation – Dubai;
>
> » **MQA** – Malaysian Qualifications Agency – Malaysia;
>
> » **OAAA** – Oman Academic Accreditation Authority – Oman;
>
> » **QAA** – The Quality Assurance Agency for Higher Education – UK;
>
> » **TEQSA** – Tertiary Education Quality and Standards Agency – Australia.

The different bodies approach quality assurance in different ways and will have different requirements and expectations for TNE provision. Example 3.1 outlines of the UK's approach.

Example 3.1

QAA and the quality assurance of UK TNE

The QAA has overseen the quality assurance of TNE since its establishment in 1997 as part of its aim to safeguard standards and improve the quality of UK higher education, wherever it is located. Traditionally, the review process has been two-fold. TNE was reviewed as part of the main institutional review process, guided, since 2012, by the *Quality Code*. In addition, there were TNE-focused review processes carried out using a country-based approach, guided by the *Transnational Education Review: Handbook*. Recent country reviews include Hong Kong (2018); the Republic of Ireland (2017); and Greece and Cyprus (2015). The QAA play a significant role in international quality assurance

→

networks and works closely with other quality assurance agencies. At the time of writing, the establishment of the Office for Students (OfS) is changing how quality assurance is operationalised and a consultation in October 2019 sought feedback to scope the future form of a UK TNE quality enhancement system.

See: Trifiro (2019); Smith (2017) and the QAA's Transnational Education Review: www.qaa.ac.uk/international/transnational-education- review

One of the complexities of TNE is that it is conducted across different jurisdictions and often needs to meet the requirements of both the degree-awarding institutions and the local regulator. While partners may share a focus on safeguarding standards and protecting students, they can have different (sometimes culturally driven) understandings of what quality is, resulting in *'the development of varied mechanisms for its determination and measurement'* (Lim, 2010, p 215).

TNE providers can also find themselves caught between two regulatory systems, which are not complementary. In her article exploring the working lives of academics at an Australian IBC in Malaysia, Dobos (2011) outlines how the campus was audited by both the MQA (Malaysian Qualifications Agency) and the AUQA (Australian Universities Quality Agency, dissolved in 2011 and replaced by the TEQSA, Tertiary Education Quality and Standards Agency). The IBC needed to satisfy the needs of both agencies, which had different foci; one interviewee commented that while the MQA *'are looking at things from the Malaysian point of view, especially at compliance with local legislation, AUQA is more holistic, looking at the intent and the spirit. It is like having two masters and you are trying to please both'* (Dobos, 2011, p 30). The time and resources required to meet the different quality assurance needs can impact negatively on partner institutions, leaving little opportunity to engage in enhancement activities (Lim, 2010, p 221), or lead to changes in the curriculum that are alien to the provider, eg the requirement of the Chinese Ministry of Education to have 'patriotic education' courses in foreign programmes (Healey, 2015).

Sometimes, however, engagement with local agencies can positively change the nature of the relationship between the awarding institution and their partner, particularly as TNE partnerships mature.

Example 3.2

Developing TNE relationships through local accreditation

In her study on academic work in an IBC, L Smith (2009) noted that the initial relationship between the home campus and the IBC was 'parent' and 'child'. Those at the IBC, in the Middle East, resented somewhat those at the Australian home campus, who managed the quality assurance process yet were perceived to not *'really understand what is going on in UAE'* (p 472). As the IBC grew, the relationship improved, and part of the improvement was the resultant local accreditation. In order to gain accreditation, the IBC had to operate as an autonomous institution, with control of its own assessment practices and providing its own degrees. The home institution had to change its role as well, moving from an internal quality controller to an external assessor. This shift in relationship had a positive impact on communication and resulted in a more professional and respectful relationship.

Institutional approaches

For the degree-awarding institution, the approach to quality assurance for TNE might duplicate existing institutional quality procedures within the home context. A defining feature of German TNE, for example, is that the design and contents of the curricula are *'developed and monitored according to the quality standards of German universities'* (Ashour, 2018, p 8). While importing countries may also require local regulation, the responsibility for the operationalisation of quality assurance often lies with the degree-awarding institution. The degree-awarding institutions, and the exporting nations in which they reside, are driving the globalisation of higher education, rather than TNE driving globalisation 'at home' (Lim et al, 2016, p 538). When the power rests with the degree-awarding institution, the experience of quality assurance is quite different if you are from there or its partner, or if you are at the home campus rather than the IBC (Yokoyama, 2011).

Quality procedures are sometimes overlaid with additional oversight from an awarding institution link person, who supports the quality process through visits to the partner organisation, approval and moderation of assessments, meeting with TNE students, and facilitating staff development opportunities for partner staff. These link roles (often called a link tutor or partner lead) are important to the success of the TNE partnership, and the link person is expected to have an understanding of not only the awarding institution's assessment and quality processes and approaches to curriculum design and delivery, but also of the partner requirements and the local context. The implementation of quality assurance is often not straightforward.

Critical issues

The challenges in implementing quality assurance

While there are national agencies to guide quality assurance, senior managers need to consider how institutional structures and policies support its implementation. In an interview study with 12 participants (programme, course and module leaders, and local tutors) engaged in Chinese–British partnerships, Bordogna (2019) found two recurring themes in relation to the operationalisation of quality assurance: time and cultural difference. In terms of time, participants noted the challenges of different non-coinciding calendars, lack of time for conversations, time differences and their impact on the organisation of assessment, turnaround times for assessment and giving feedback, and a lack of time due to other responsibilities. In relation to cultural differences, participants spoke of a lack of identification with the degree-awarding institution, different expectations of the programme and the maintenance of standards, and a lack of regard for agreed marking schemes and assessment protocols. Bordogna argues that senior managers need to become more aware of the challenges of implementing quality assurance in TNE and create safe spaces where challenges and concerns can be shared to improve and enhance TNE.

Critical question for practice

» What are your institutional guidelines for quality assurance in relation to TNE and are senior managers helping implement these effectively?

There are challenges in enacting quality procedures and some of these challenges stem from a focus on equivalence that is often a feature of quality assurance in TNE.

Questions of equivalence in quality assurance

Questions of equivalence and comparability between programmes offered in the degree-awarding institutions and in the host institutions feature in much writing on quality assurance in TNE (eg Lim et al, 2016; Smith, 2010; Stella, 2006). Guiding documents may refer explicitly to equivalence; for example the University Quality Assurance International Board (UQAIB) uses an 'Equivalency Validation Model' to assess the quality equivalence of provision in Dubai in relation to the degree-awarding institution (QAA, 2018a, p 5) and the Australian TESQA requires that *'student learning outcomes are equivalent to those for the same or a cognate course of study when delivered by the higher education provider'* (cited in Lim et al, 2016, p 530).

But what does equivalent mean? Equivalency is contentious, in education generally, but especially in TNE (Lim et al, 2016, p 538). Sharp (2017) suggests that, in relation to the quality of TNE, it is useful to distinguish between:

» academic standards – *'the depth, breadth and complexity of the knowledge and skills, of which a candidate has demonstrated possession, at the conclusion of his or her programme of study'* (Sharp, 2017, p 139);

» learning opportunities – *'formal teaching, the provision of learning resources such as libraries and information technology laboratories, students support and guidance as well as classrooms, leisure facilities and extra-curricular activities'* (Sharp, 2017, p 142).

Sharp argues (2017, p 147) that, in terms of quality assurance and our confidence in the higher education provided, it is important that there are equivalent (or common) standards in TNE and domestic contexts, but that there might be differences in terms of the learning opportunities.

Yet, even this distinction raises questions about whose academic standards we are assuring (Sharp, 2017). There is no one set of universal standards, and as shown, it can be challenging when more than one set of national standards is being applied. Academic standards themselves are socially and culturally situated; the disciplinary knowledge on which standards are based is located within a particular academic community and there are no concrete rules as to what counts as 'legitimate' knowledge (Sharp, 2017, pp 141–2). The work of Waters and Leung (2017) critically examines the mobility of knowledge. They argue in TNE knowledge is assumed to be generic and ideas, theories and empirical realities can be unproblematically transplanted from one nation into another. There is indeed a tendency in TNE to use an identical curriculum as a *'safe and less resource intensive approach'* (Lim et al, 2016, p 537) to assure equivalence. This is what McBurnie and Ziguras (2007, p 51) term *'packaging curriculum'*, or centrally producing a curriculum that can be offered in different locations. The benefits of this approach are the consistency and clarity about what is taught, certainty over its quality, and level of control that the awarding institution has over the curriculum delivered in its name. Coleman (2003, p 367) argues that with shared curriculum and standard approaches to marking, the variations in terms of the distance between the TNE partners, staff and student demographics, preferences for teaching and learning, staffing arrangements and the experiential relationship with the programme (which I understand to result from its political, social, cultural, institutional and historical context) mean that, in TNE, *'academic equivalency and educational congruency simply cannot be presumed'* (Coleman, 2003, p 359) and that a *'blunt copying of curricula does not seem a wise or feasible strategy'* (Waterval et al, 2015, p 78).

In my own work, I have found it useful to draw on work from translation studies to understand what equivalence should be sought in TNE provision (Smith, 2010). Translation scholars Nida and Taber (1974, pp 200–1) distinguish between formal and dynamic equivalence. Formal equivalence is the closest equivalent to the source language. In TNE, that might be an exact copy of programmes already offered by the degree-awarding body. A completely transferred programme, however, might be difficult for TNE students to decipher and can create inequalities in terms of background understanding and experience. In contrast, dynamic equivalence aims to achieve the same impact on the target audience as the original had on the source. This allows for local adaptation, while meeting academic standards. In TNE, the adaptation work needed to make sure the curriculum makes sense (and achieve dynamic equivalence) is often undertaken by the local partners; but this additional work is often not articulated or recognised in terms of equivalence and in the measuring of academic standards (Lim et al, 2016, p 537). Rather than *post hoc* patching by the partner to facilitate TNE student learning, there is a case for more collaborative approaches to programme design institutionally, and to quality assurance generally at a national level.

Collaborative approaches to quality assurance

As noted in Chapter 1, there are movements in TNE towards more collaborative and partnership-based models. Collaborative approaches to quality assurance, and ultimately quality enhancement, are also possible. In terms of programme design and approval, collaborative approaches between staff from the degree-awarding and the delivering institutions could foster shared understanding and ultimately better student experiences. In doctoral work looking at quality assurance of UK–Sri Lankan

TNE, Williams (2018, pp 118–19) identified the following competencies, required for all engaged in TNE to ensure effective quality assurance:

» technical knowledge (eg understanding the regulations that govern provision);

» relational (eg diplomacy, respecting others, collaborative problem solving);

» intercultural (eg not making assumptions, respecting cultural sensitivities);

» communication (eg effective communication face-to-face and online).

I would argue that these competencies are applicable to all roles within TNE; they can be developed both through training (discussed further in Chapter 5), and through experience. In relation to quality assurance, at a basic level, even sharing a quality assurance timeline can be a useful tool '*to open up debate and discussion*' about roles and responsibilities (Hughes, 2011, p 25) and regular face-to-face meetings can support mutual learning (Lamers-Reeuwijk et al, 2019). There are, however, more fundamental changes that could be made to foster more inclusive approaches to curriculum design and delivery, which recognise, for example, the importance of communities of practice (Keay et al, 2014); TNE curriculum design frameworks (Clarke et al, 2016); or the reconfiguration of TNE boundaries to support collaboration.

Example 3.3

Reconfiguring boundaries in TNE teaching teams

In Keevers et al's (2019) case study institutions, quality assurance shaped learning, teaching and assessment. It was based on a home–host relationship, which paired subject coordinators from both settings; the home institution played the role of 'quality assurer' and checking and monitoring were emphasised. While quality systems were supportive of co-operation and communication, these did not always happen in practice and there was no sharing of experiences across the wider teaching teams. Their wider project used participatory action learning (PAL) to explore aspects of professional practice development across the different delivery sites. Following engagement in the PAL projects, TNE relationships were reconfigured and expanded to support the development of more inclusive transnational teaching teams and intercultural communities of practice. The benefits of this reconfiguration included enhanced relationships, improved collaboration and dialogue, the co-development of curricula and quality measures, and a different view of quality assurance.

If the power for quality assurance rests with the degree-awarding institution, then it is in the hands of those institutions to create the environment where partners can be included in programme review and approval stages (Dass, 2019, p 173) to engender collective responsibility for the quality of TNE provided.

Critical question for practice

» How do you currently work with your TNE partners? How could your collaboration be enhanced?

There are also movements towards more cross-border collaboration in relation to quality assurance. While there are calls for a commonly accepted framework for quality standards in TNE (Choudaha and Edelstein, 2014), Trifiro (2019) argues that in the foreseeable future there is unlikely to be such a shared set of standards and processes (given the differences between national systems). The movement should be, and is, in the direction of more cross-border and inter-agency collaboration. Trifiro (2019) outlines examples of international initiatives that have sought to develop further co-operation, including groups and networks, and projects and initiatives.

Initiatives, which bring national agencies closer together, help develop mutual understandings and trust, and mitigate the risk of TNE provision being caught between conflicting quality assurance requirements. They also recognise that while TNE can be a high-risk activity that challenges quality assurance, it is also an innovative form of higher education that can bring real benefits to students (Trifiro, 2019); students, their motivations, expectations and experiences, are the focus of the next chapter.

Summary

- Questions of quality are key in TNE, but quality is a slippery term in higher education and quality assurance is particularly complicated when working transnationally.
- Quality assurance is enacted globally (through UNESCO *Guidelines* and international networks), nationally (through national agencies) and institutionally (often led by a link person/quality assessor).

- Quality assurance of TNE can be challenging due to the requirements to work across jurisdictions (sometimes fulfilling the requirements of more than one agency), the power inequalities between partners, and their cultural differences.

- Questions of equivalence feature large in TNE, but equivalence does not have to mean exact copies of degree-awarding institutions' programmes delivered elsewhere, which can create inequalities. Local adaptation is often needed to engender equivalent experiences.

- Collaborative approaches to quality assurance (both nationally and institutionally) can develop shared understandings and collective responsibility for the quality of TNE.

Useful texts

Bordogna, C M (2019). Are Degree-Awarding Institutions Doing Enough to Support the Implementation of Quality Assurance in Transnational Higher Education Partnerships? *Journal of Studies in International Education.* [online] Available at: https://journals.sagepub.com/doi/abs/10.1177/1028315319888458 (accessed 16 January 2020).

Claudia Bordogna's article outlines the challenges of following national guidelines and implementing quality assurance.

ENQA (2015) *The Cooperation in Cross-Border Higher Education: A Toolkit for Quality Assurance Agencies.* [online] Available at: https://enqa.eu/indirme/papers-and-reports/occasional-papers/QACHE%20Toolkit_web.pdf (accessed 16 January 2020).

The Cooperation in Cross-Border Higher Education: A Toolkit for Quality Assurance Agencies provides an overview as to how quality assurance agencies can implement the UNESCO Guidelines for Quality Provision in Cross-Border Higher Education.

Trifiro, F (2019). The Importance of Cross-Border Cooperation in the Quality Assurance of TNE: A Comparative Overview of National Approaches to TNE, *Higher Education Evaluation and Development.* [online] Available at: www.emerald.com/insight/content/doi/10.1108/HEED-12-2018-0030/full/html (accessed 16 January 2020).

Fabrizio Trifiro's article on inter-agency cooperation provides an overview of how national quality assurance agencies from major exporting and importing countries assure TNE and how, increasingly, they work together.

Who are TNE students?

In the previous two chapters, I have introduced the motivations for practitioners, institutions and nations to engage in TNE, and the global drivers that facilitate TNE, before turning my attention to how the quality of the TNE offering is assured. Here, I focus on students and their experiences, addressing the following questions.

» What do we know about TNE students?

» What are the 'push' and 'pull' factors that motivate their engagement in TNE and what do they expect from it?

» What are TNE students' experiences of their learning environment and learning opportunities?

As discussed in Chapter 1, it is difficult to state categorically who studies on TNE programmes because there is no standard approach internationally for recording TNE student numbers. While some countries do systematically collect data on TNE, others do not, making it very hard to present a global picture. Even when countries have robust systems, their systems are not always aligned, as the example shows.

Example 4.1

Differences in approaches to data collection

The UK has a centralised system for collecting data on TNE activity through its Aggregate Offshore Record (the AOR). The AOR is a report that UK universities complete and return to the Higher Education Statistical Agency (HESA). It captures data on the number of students studying for degrees wholly outside the UK, who are either registered with the reporting higher education provider or who are studying for an award of the reporting provider (HESA, 2016). The AOR differentiates between programmes delivered in a partnership framework (eg franchise, twinning, validation) and those delivered through an IBC (Levatino, 2015). In contrast, the Department for Education and Training (DET) in Australia collects data on students enrolled on offshore campuses (which includes twinning arrangements and IBCs) and students engaged in distance and online learning (McNamara and Knight, 2015). The Australian data has information about TNE students' countries of birth as well as the country in which they are studying, while the UK data reports only on location of the TNE arrangement, making the impact of country of origin on TNE choices difficult to assess (Levatino, 2015).

Rather than an internationally comparative picture, you can learn about TNE students through country profiles, eg:

» McNamara and Knight (2015) profile 10 host countries (Botswana, Egypt, Hong Kong, Jordan, Malaysia, Mauritius, Mexico, Turkey, UAE and Vietnam) and three sending country profiles (UK, Australia and Germany).

Alternatively, individual countries might produce an overview of their own engagement in TNE, eg:

» the UUKi (2018) report on the scale of UK higher education TNE;

» the Australian DET Research Snapshot of offshore delivery of Australian higher education (Department of Education and Training, 2018).

These reports present a statistical picture, which generally includes the number of students enrolled, the programmes they are taking, and their level. To better understand the potential TNE student market, the British Council ran a survey of prospective TNE students, which was administered at international education exhibitions and through online education portals and email invitations, between 2007 and 2012, where 150,000 students responded. In addition, 13 interviews with then current students, alumni and administrators were carried out. The findings were written into a report entitled: *Portrait of a Transnational Education Student* (2012b); Example 4.2 summarises the key findings.

Example 4.2

Portrait of a TNE student

The analysis of the prospective TNE student survey data paints a picture of the kinds of student who consider TNE as a way of accessing higher education, reporting data on age distribution, employment status and subject interest of prospective TNE students. It shows that 40 per cent of those over 40 consider a TNE programme, suggesting its attractiveness to mature learners or those seeking professional development. Potential (postgraduate and undergraduate) TNE students are likely to be full-time students or already employed. Business and engineering degrees are popular for potential undergraduate students, with business, social studies, engineering and technology, English language and media studies popular for postgraduates. The potential students were more interested in whether the programme was relevant, recognised and would impact on their future career aspirations than in the reputation of the awarding institution. Prospective TNE students were seeking flexibility, quality teaching, and employ-ability. The student experience was of less importance when choosing a TNE programme, although in the interviews with current students, experience was something those students wished they had explored further. The British Council (2012b, p 25) concluded that TNE students are: *'goal-orientated, and highly motivated to progress along a premeditated career path'.*

Critical questions for practice

» Are your TNE students like the ones profiled in the example above?

» If there are differences, are they a reflection of the context of your specific TNE, or of the evolution of TNE more generally since 2012?

Portrait of a Transnational Education Student (British Council, 2012b) notes that while there are differences between these globally spread potential TNE students, there were defining features in terms of needs, priorities and outlooks that made the TNE student community distinctive. We can learn about this distinctiveness through the case studies that report on TNE students' motivations, expectations and experiences.

Motivations and expectations

The portrait of a TNE student example provides some of the motivations for students to engage in TNE; namely, convenience, flexibility, employability, quality, time and relevance. In this next section, motivations and expectations will be explored through reference to the 'push-pull' factors for TNE student choice and the national and insti-tutional motivations outlined in Chapter 2.

Push-pull theory

Push-pull theory has been used as a way to better understand what influences international students' choice of destination for their higher education (Mazzarol and Soutar, 2002). The students' decision on where to engage is made through a combination of 'push' and 'pull' factors. 'Push' factors that may encourage a student to leave their home country to study include difficulty in accessing the programme at home, international course deemed to be of better quality, or an intention to migrate on graduation (Mazzarol and Soutar, 2002, p 88). 'Pull' factors that encourage the student to take up study in a specific country might include knowledge and awareness of the country; influence of friends and family; cost of living; and geographical proximity to the home country. Decisions to attend a particular institution in a different country can include: its reputation for quality and higher-quality teachers; recognition of qualifications; alumni base and links with other institutions known by the student (Mazzarol and Soutar, 2002, p 89). Here the decision is between domestic or international education.

Push-pull theory has also been used to explore student choice with specific reference to TNE, albeit in a revised form (eg Ahmad and Buchanan, 2016; Fang and Wang, 2014). Here students have three choices, not two, as I have shown in Figure 4.1.

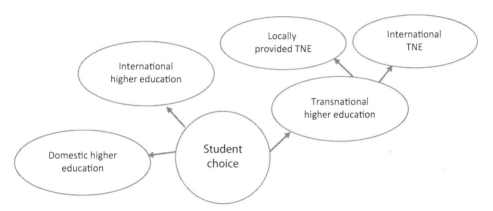

Figure 4.1 Student choice for higher education.

In relation to the choice of TNE, as Fang and Wang (2014, p 477) note, a student's choice:

Results from the pull factors related to transnational higher education and the push factors related to overseas higher education and domestic higher education. Pull factors are all positive. Push factors will be either positive or negative.

Students can choose domestic higher education, to study abroad ('international' education), or transnational education (Fang and Wang, 2014). To recognise that student may cross borders to engage in TNE, I have added that if they choose TNE, they have the option of TNE that is locally provided, or to travel to a different country for 'international' TNE.

In the next sections, some of the many push and pull factors will be explored through a selection of published reports and research on students' motivations for enrolling on TNE programmes.

Pull of TNE

There are many pull factors that can motivate students to engage in a TNE programme. Mok and Han (2016) carried out a questionnaire study of students' motivations to engage in TNE programmes at two Sino-foreign co-operation universities in China (n=69 students), and contrast their responses with students who were, or would be, studying overseas, outside of China (n=72 students). The findings show, in relation to the pull of TNE, that the low tuition fees and living costs were a reason for choosing the TNE programme, with 51 per cent of TNE students noting this in contrast to 11 per cent of students engaged in or considering moving overseas to study.

A further finding suggests that those engaged in TNE programmes were more concerned about their future job prospects than those who were (or were considering studying) overseas, and they paid more attention to whether their degrees would be recognised by future employers (87 per cent for TNE students; 79 per cent for overseas students). Prospective TNE students might do more research into potential programmes, like this student:

Before I applied, I referred to the official website of the Ministry of Education and asked nearly all the friends/relatives who know my university about the validity of the certificates issued by this university.

(Mok and Han, 2016, p 382)

If a TNE provider can assure prospective students that their awards will be attractive to local employers, then this may represent a key pull factor. This focus on employ-ability has been identified by researchers in other countries. Pyvis and Chapman (2007) found that Malaysian students saw their Australian TNE in Malaysia as a means of gaining access to employment in multinational corporations. This driver was contrasted with the motivations expressed by the non-Malaysian students (from countries including China, Canada and Kenya) who were seeking a more international education, to *'set them on the road to being "international" beings'* (Pyvis and Chapman, 2007, p 236). Here the pull of the international TNE programme is combined with the pull of the host country (see below). TNE as a stepping stone into future employment or further study is discussed later in this chapter.

A further factor, noted in Mok and Han's work (2016), is access to an English-language environment. For those studying overseas, 100 per cent cited access to an English environment as one of their main reasons for choosing their programme. Indeed, these same students also stated that this access was a key reason for also not accessing TNE programmes, because although the programme would often be delivered and assessed in English, the environment would not be English. Yet, those engaged in TNE did value its English medium, with 83 per cent citing it as a motivation for engagement. While these TNE students were not studying in an English-speaking country, the programme enabled them to practise English:

I chose to study here simply because all the courses here are taught in English. I could thus practice English speaking and listening skills in daily life, which may facilitate my application and acclimatisation with western cultures.

(Mok and Han, 2016, p 378)

For many contemplating TNE, the pull of English is strong. The English-language medium dominates TNE.

Critical issues

The dominance of English in TNE

The internationalisation of higher education (of which TNE is a part) has been, as Phan argues, '*institutionalised around a linguistic preference for English*' (2017, p 16). While there are examples of TNE offered in other languages (eg Debowski, 2005; Wilkins and Urbanovič, 2014), for most, TNE is an '*English-only package*' (Phan, 2017, p 84). While students desire to learn in English, the use of English only, irrespective of location, raises its own challenges. In her study of students engaged in an American medical degree in Qatar, Kane (2014) observed that students struggled with 'linguistic gaps' and alien cultural references as they engaged with their American medical curriculum. With time, the students developed their English language, but at the expense, some felt, of their Arabic. When the students found themselves on their clinical placements, they struggled again to translate their American training back into their Arabian contexts. In a counter-example, Waters and Leung (2013) found that their 'immobile international' TNE students in Hong Kong lacked the 'mobility capital' that students who travelled to the UK to study acquired. The quality of the proficiency in English gained through TNE and through overseas study was different; TNE students were disadvantaged by this experience. With its aims to widen access to higher education, TNE is also, of course, disadvantaging students who cannot make the English requirements necessary to engage in TNE programmes.

According to Mok and Han (2016), while other motivators such as quality, qualification recognition and the English environment are important for engaging in TNE, when compared with overseas study, the lower cost of TNE programmes is a major pull factor.

Pull of the host country

As noted in Chapter 2, host countries might develop a strategy to encourage international education providers to set up in their country. By attracting high-quality and reputable universities who offer specialised courses, TNE programmes draw in domestic and international students. While these factors relate to the pull of the international provider and its impact on student recruitment, TNE students' motivation to study might also be a result of the pull of the host country. The portrayal of the host country, as a destination of choice, can be seen particularly in relation to education hubs.

Example 4.3

Motivation to study at IBCs in Malaysia

Ahmad and Buchanan (2016, 2017) carried out research into the factors that influence students' decisions to enrol on TNE programmes at IBCs in Malaysia. Their research reports on qualitative interviews with 24 international (non-Malaysian) students (Ahmad and Buchanan, 2016) and a survey with 218 students and 18 further interviews (Ahmad and Buchanan). Their work highlights the importance of the perceived positive features of Malaysia as a place to study. The attractive features of TNE in Malaysia include:

» the geographical location of Malaysia, its distance from the students' homes, and a more familiar climate;

» the lower cost of living and possibilities to work;

» the comparative cost of study at Malaysian IBCs when compared to study elsewhere;

» the perception of Malaysia as a safe place to live and study: politically stable, with a low crime rate and free from most natural disasters;

» the perception of Malaysia as an exciting place to live with a range of social events and leisure activities, an ethnically diverse and friendly learning environment;

» an environment, as a modern Islamic state, that is culturally and religiously closer to some students' experiences than Western countries;

» the widespread use of English and accessible visa and immigration system.

The attractiveness of the host country can influence students' decision making in terms of destination choice for TNE.

Push factors from overseas

The motivation to engage in TNE programmes rather than to undertake study at the home campus or degree-awarding institution might be a result of factors that push against leaving the home country, and in many ways stand in contra-distinction to the host country's pull factors; for example, the cost of studying in some countries can be prohibitive for many students considering international higher education.

While studying complete degree programmes abroad and far from home might be attractive to younger and more affluent students, not all potential students have sufficient financial or personal circumstances to do this. TNE can be more attractive due to accessibility and its often-part-time nature, which means that students can engage in study as well as work and maintain a family, as Pyvis and Chapman's (2005) report on Australian TNE programmes delivered in Hong Kong and Singapore shows. This research indicated that the visa restrictions associated with working as a student in Australia were also a push factor away from completing a degree overseas.

Visa regulations can have a negative impact on student mobility. The complexity of the visa process and access to post-study work visas can discourage students from studying abroad. In the UK, for example, the abolition of the post-study work visa led to a dramatic decline in the number of Indian students coming to the UK (Kennedy, 2019); and while some of these Indian students may have taken up studies in countries such as the USA, Canada or Australia, where post-study work arrangements are more generous (O'Carroll, 2018), some may have opted to enrol on UK TNE programmes instead, as India remains a significant host of UK TNE (UUKi, 2018).

The political situation might also mean that some overseas destinations are less attractive to students. The events on 11 September 2001 (9/11) have influenced some students' decisions about where to study. There was, for example, a decrease in students from the Middle East applying to study in the USA following 9/11 because they felt, as Muslims, they would not be welcome there; concurrently, Malaysia, which has positioned itself as an education hub, saw an increase in Middle Eastern students choosing TNE in Malaysia as a destination where they would feel safe (Sirat, 2008).

Example 4.4

IBCs in post-Brexit plans

Anticipating a fall in student recruitment to the UK from the European mainland following the UK's decision to leave the European Union, some UK universities are considering establishing a physical presence in Europe through an IBC. In addition to attracting European students, a European-based IBC could also maintain established partnerships and make access to European funding easier (Havergal, 2018). Lawton and Tsiligiris (2018) contend, however, that for most UK universities, IBCs are not part of their internationalisation strategies, and that Europe would not be a particularly good market as the UK would be competing with local, high-quality higher education with free or subsidised tuition.

Push of domestic higher education

TNE students might be motivated to engage in TNE courses because domestic higher education provision does not meet their needs, pushing them towards other kinds of provision.

In the UAE, federal higher education is available primarily for the Emirati population. The growing numbers of expatriates living in the Emirates wanted access to higher education and IBCs were established to target this market. The UAE currently has 37 IBCs, mainly situated in free zones in Dubai, but with both Abu Dhabi and Ras Al Khaimah hosting IBCs too (QAA, 2014). While it was a lack of provision that pushed students to TNE in the UAE, foreign education providers have been encouraged to come to the UAE by their governments, primarily through the establishment of free zones which offer foreign providers incentives relating to ownership, facilities, tax exemptions, profit and capital repatriation, and the regulatory environment (QAA, 2014). The model has been so successful that the UAE has become an education hub; no longer catering solely to the expatriate community who had few UAE-based alternatives for higher education, but also serving international students who are attracted by the pull of the TNE host country, and TNE more generally.

The domestic market might not offer the range of specialised subjects that students want to study. For developing higher education systems, there might not yet be the advanced, specialised and higher-level study that contributes to ongoing professional development and upskilling of the local population. A TNE programme could be the only way to gain access to training in a mode of study that is accessible. In her study of mature-aged learners on TNE programmes in Singapore, Hoare (2012) found that experienced professionals who had missed out on promotion due to lack of a degree were given a 'second chance' through TNE. The example below, on TNE in Malaysia, suggests similar benefits.

Example 4.5

Malaysian nurse engagement in TNE top-up degrees

Arunasalam (2016) explored Malaysian nurses' motivations for engaging in TNE programmes. In Malaysia, as in many other countries, there has been a shift in nurse education from a diploma qualification to a degree. There was a lack of part-time or flexible off-campus provision within the Malaysian higher education system to enable practising nurses to upgrade their qualifications. To meet this need, the Malaysian Nursing Board encouraged collaborations between Malaysian hospitals, private and public higher education institutions and foreign higher education institutions (namely the UK and Australia) to provide post-registration top-up nursing degree programmes. Arunasalam (2016) found that TNE offered a flexible means for nurses to gain graduate status. Other motivations included the higher status of a Western degree, the financial incentives to study and the promotion opportunities available on completion. These motivations, which are individualistic and extrinsic, were more important than the desire to deepen learning or change practice.

There is unlikely to be a single reason why students choose to enrol on a TNE programme. In reality, their choice will be the culmination of a complex interplay of push and pull factors that will be influenced by the students' backgrounds, previous experiences, geographical location and personal and professional aspirations. Having a better understanding of these motivations and expectations will help those engaged in TNE to provide a better experience.

Critical question for practice

» What do you know of your students' motivations for engaging in TNE?

TNE student experiences

Given the reporting difficulties noted earlier and the fact that TNE students are often not represented in national satisfaction surveys (eg TNE students are currently not included in the UK's National Student Survey [NSS]), there is limited research on TNE students' experiences (O'Mahony, 2014, p 36). Research into TNE student experiences is usually small scale (often related to a single programme) and country specific. Given the diversity of students engaged in TNE, with their different motivations and expectations, operating in different countries, under different modes of TNE, means that attempts to generalise the TNE student experience would be impossible anyway.

Yet there are areas that relate to the TNE student experience more generally. The first concerns experiences of learning, teaching and assessment and this is discussed in Chapter 5. Here, I look at TNE students and their learning environment before exploring TNE student affiliation.

Experiences of TNE learning environments and educational opportunities

While the Ningbo, China campus is a mirror of the campus in Nottingham, UK (BBC, 2015), most TNE students do not experience exact replicas of the home institution's learning environments. The library might be smaller and there might not be the equivalent sports facilities, student services, clubs or societies. Research carried out by the QAA found that UK TNE students at IBCs in Dubai felt their experience could be improved if they had access to a more comparable student experience to the students at the home campus, including access to a broad range of student services and extra-curricular activities (QAA, 2018a, p 24). The different opportunities might impact negatively on students.

Critical issues

TNE and the reproduction of social (dis)advantage

Waters and Leung (2012), looking at top-up degrees in Hong Kong, showed that while the students in their research had sought out TNE as a means to access higher education (when they did not meet the entry requirements for a local Hong Kong university), the degree did not always provide them with the *'entry-ticket'* into a job on graduation and could lead to *'reduced privileges*' in relation to local universities (Waters and Leung, 2012, p 4). With reduced access to activities and resources linked to campus life (eg computing and library facilities, halls of residence, sports and social activities, students' union and work experience), TNE can, Waters and Leung (2012, pp 5–6) argue, reproduce patterns of (local) disadvantage and reinforce social inequality and social exclusion. They conclude that although TNE provides students opportunities to access higher education that would not be available otherwise, the opportunities can be a '*double-edged sword*' (2012, p 6).

For the students in the Critical Issue above, access to employment was a key motivator for engaging in a TNE degree and was not always found on completion. One area where TNE students appear to be disadvantaged is in the development of employability skills. Mellors-Bourne et al (2015) outline several reasons why this might be the case, including limited access to careers guidance, internships, work placements and employer engagement in curriculum design and delivery of TNE programmes. Given that many TNE programmes are vocational in nature, the lack of opportunities to further develop employability skills could well disadvantage TNE students in comparison to students based at the degree-awarding institution and also raises questions as to what job market the TNE programmes are developing them to enter. This does not affect all TNE, however; the example below provides an illustration about how university–industry partnerships can be developed to meet the needs of the host country.

Example 4.6

Education for aviation

In 2018, the University of South Wales (USW) opened an IBC in Dubai specialising in aviation and meeting the increasing demand for aviation mechanics in the Middle East and Asia through a suite of undergraduate and postgraduate programmes. Some undergraduate degree programmes incorporate a period of industrial training, which contributes towards achieving the requirements to be a licensed aircraft maintenance engineer. The USW has partnered with local industries to support the training element. The programmes in Dubai mirror those on offer in the UK and students can move between campuses, allowing students to start their degree in Dubai, do the second year in Wales and then return to Dubai to complete (see: WECD/iUUK, 2018, pp 44–5).

As shown in Chapter 3, there has long been an emphasis on equivalence in terms of the curriculum (eg the content, materials, resources, and the learning, teaching and assessment methods), but now comparability extends beyond this to student experiences more broadly.

For those students engaged in TNE where the degree-awarding institution has no physical presence in the host country, there is perhaps less of an expectation that the facilities will be the same as they are provided by the delivery partner, yet there is an expectation that there will be access to the resources necessary to follow the pro-gramme. Through advances in information and communication technologies (ICT), students, with accessible platforms and stable internet, should be able to access a vast array of learning resources, guidance, support and online training to support their learning. While students enrolled in distance learning or local partner delivery models of TNE may not expect '*a branch campus-type student experience*', they may feel, as TNE students studying on a collaborative partnership in Singapore did, that more could be done to enhance their experiences in relation to strengthening their sense of belonging to the awarding institution (QAA, 2018, p 24); affiliation is important for TNE students.

Finding affiliation in TNE

Much work around supporting transition into and enhancing students' experiences at university is connected with developing a sense of belonging or affiliation to the higher education institution where they are enrolled (O'Keeffe, 2013). But where does TNE student affiliation lie? Is it to their course, department or disciplinary area? Is it to the degree-awarding institution? In the case of the IBC, are students seeking to belong to the overarching corporate brand (eg New York University) or specifically to one of its international entities (eg New York University, Abu Dhabi); what these campuses offer will be different (Wilkins and Huisman, 2013) and hence what the students belong to differs too. Students might be able to move between campuses, as shown in the USW example above.

While IBCs have the advantage of physical spaces in which, at least, markers of insti-tutional identity can be shared, for many other forms of TNE (eg franchise, validation and articulation arrangements), connections with the degree-awarding institution may be much less obvious and may need to be actively fostered (Smith, 2017, pp 68–9 provides examples). Students who do not spend time at the degree-awarding insti-tution or have little connection with students at their degree-awarding institution, nor with students working with other partners in other parts of the world can feel isolated or excluded from the wider university community. This apparent exclusion can be made worse when there is no physical space that belongs to the TNE students, leaving them unable to function as a 'normal university student' (Waters and Leung, 2012). Affiliation, then, might not be with the degree-awarding institution, but rather with the partner. Fang and Wang (2014), for example, found that the ranking of the host university (here a Chinese university) had a major influence on students' reasons to select a particular programme. TNE students might choose a programme because of the reputation of the partner and seek to be part of that community, rather than on the merits of the degree-awarding institution.

Example 4.7

Articulation students

A feature of Chinese TNE is articulation programmes, which operate on a system of a period in China followed by time in the foreign university (eg 2+2, 3+1 or 1+1). This model involves students physically moving to complete their studies, and therefore undergoing a period of adjustment, into the university system and into the foreign environment. In their study of articulation students' experiences in Australia, Dai and Garcia (2019) found that while some of their participants felt they have adjusted well to study in Australia, some did not feel that they belonged there at all, experiencing isolation, homesickness, language and learning barriers.

Feeling affiliation to a university is important in relation to the student experience and there are knock-on effects of fostering positive TNE student experiences.

Knock-on effects of positive TNE student experiences

As alumni of the degree-awarding institution, former TNE students can contribute to the development of their *alma mater*. Beyond the financial benefits of donations, TNE alumni can help to establish networks in different countries which support global graduate employability, as well as facilitate the recruitment of further students (Miller, 2013). Another positive effect of good TNE student experiences for the degree-awarding institution is the student choosing to continue their studies at their main campus or to progress to postgraduate study in the UK (HEFCE, 2014). These are examples of the connection between a TNE student and the degree-awarding institution. TNE can also foster an enduring connection between the TNE student and the exporting country.

TNE students may not always feel a strong affinity with, or even understanding of, the exporting country (Mellors-Bourne, 2017, p 46); yet, it has been shown that enrolment on a TNE degree can lead to an increase in skilled migration into the country that exported the education. Levatino posits, based on scrutiny of Australian Department of Immigration and Citizenship and Australian DIIRSTE data, that TNE acts more as *'a magnet'* for people to come to the originating country; her research shows *'a positive and statistically significant association between skilled immigration into Australia and offshore* [TNE] *enrolment in Australian higher education in the previous year'* (Levatino, 2015, p 114). While she cannot extrapolate from her data those who came to study from those who came to work, there was an impact on migration into the country. This presents a paradox; in Chapter 2, one driver for national engagement in TNE was the desire to reduce 'brain drain', to stop talented young people leaving their home country to pursue higher education and never returning. It seems that TNE can have the opposite effect, rather than curbing 'brain drain', contributing to it.

Rather than seeing such mobility negatively, Mok and Han (2016) suggest a more positive interpretation of 'brain bridging' whereby former TNE students, who are potentially well placed to mediate cultures, enhance understanding and expand international networks, act as a bridge between the two countries. This supports the notion of 'soft power' influence, where trust and positive perception can be enhanced through engagement in culture and education (British Council, 2013, p 46). Such soft power influence can result in 'brain gain' (Mok and Han, 2016). When TNE students act as 'brain bridges' there are gains not just to the former TNE student in their transnational positioning, but also to both the host country and to the degree-awarding country, thus making TNE a truly mutually beneficial activity.

Summary

- It is difficult to know how many TNE students there are as countries have very different ways of counting them.

- Motivations to engage in TNE are the result of a complex interplay of 'push–pull' factors that are influenced by students' backgrounds, previous experiences, geographical location and personal and professional aspirations.

- TNE students' experiences of their learning environments and their learning opportunities are likely to differ from those of their on-campus counterparts, particularly in terms of access to facilities, extra-curricular offerings and employability opportunities.

- TNE raises questions about where TNE students find affiliation: to the degree-awarding institution, to the partner or to the programme. Where do TNE students belong?

- The ongoing benefits of positive TNE student experiences contribute to future recruitment to further study and closer ties between different cultures and countries.

Useful texts

British Council (2012) *Portrait of a Transnational Education Student*. London: British Council, Education Intelligence.

Although completed some time ago, The British Council's (2012) report Portrait of a Transnational Education Student provides an overview of potential TNE students and sheds some light on the motivations behind decisions to choose a TNE programme.

Waters, J and Leung, M (2012) Young People and Reproduction of Disadvantage through Transnational Education. *Sociological Research Online*, 17. [online] Available at: https://journals.sagepub.com/doi/full/10.5153/sro.2499 (accessed 16 January 2020).

Waters, J and Leung, M (2013) Immobile Transnationalisms? Young People and Their In Situ Experiences of 'International' Education in Hong Kong. *Urban Studies*, 50: 606–20.

Work by Johanna Waters and Maggi Leung, as part of their Hong Kong Research Grants Council and UK ESRC grant on joint initiatives between UK and Hong Kong higher education institutions, examining student and employer perspectives of TNE.

Chapter 5

TNE practitioners and their development

Who practises transnationally?

Due to the complex nature of TNE, the different activities that it encompasses, and its growth over recent years, an increasing number of higher education professionals are engaged in TNE. My own interest, as a practitioner and a researcher, has been in flying faculty teachers; however, there are many other roles associated with TNE. The list below provides an overview but is by no means exhaustive.

» Flying faculty teachers

» Local tutors

» Link tutors

» Branch campus teachers

» Branch campus managers

» Collaboration leads, based overseas

» Partnership co-ordinators

» Professional staff

» Student union representatives

» Senior managers with responsibility for international partnerships

» Administrators

» Recruiters

» Curriculum developers

» Quality assurance and accreditation professionals

» IT specialists

» Librarians

» Learning technologists and online tutors.

That so many roles have the potential to be practised transnationally reinforces the fact that higher education is increasingly global, operating beyond national boundaries. TNE brings together people with not only different professional roles, but also different cultural and educational experiences. This chapter will focus on practitioners, and will address the following questions.

» What are the key educator roles, and how do they differ?

» How is learning, teaching and assessment supported in TNE?

» How are TNE relationships managed and what impact does national culture and power have on those relationships?

» What professional development opportunities are provided to TNE practitioners?

Below, I explore in more detail just three types of staff engaged in TNE teaching practice, before looking at how relationships between such diverse professionals can be managed. While I have identified a list of TNE practitioner roles, I concentrate on educators, as this where my own research and experience lies.

Educators in TNE

Locally based tutors

Locally based tutors are staff located in the host country who provide support to the TNE students studying there. While the degree-awarding institution maintains control of assessment and curriculum development, the tuition for the programme might be carried out locally. In some cases, staff from the awarding institution may have no interaction with their TNE students at all, as all interaction is carried out locally. The benefits of having local tutors are that they are more accessible than degree-awarding institution staff, they often have similar linguistic and cultural backgrounds and can facilitate acculturation, and they are sometimes cheaper to employ (McBurnie and Ziguras, 2007, p 54).

As seen in Chapter 3, local tutors can play a crucial role in '*interpreting and adapting material to the local context and articulating learning outcomes sought by the university, including its values and culture*' (Edwards et al, 2010, p 313), but this role is often not recognised. Magne et al (2017), in their study of TNE in Hong Kong (which included UK-based staff, local tutors and students), showed that the local tutors advocated the need to localise materials, and when they were required to '*religiously deliver*' the UK materials, they felt '*they were denied the right to incorporate their voices and expertise into their teaching practice*' (Magne et al, 2017, pp 51–2).

This local tutor role can be challenging as they often do not receive any formal induction into the degree-awarding institution's culture, requirements or regulations (Edwards et al, 2010, p 313) and tend to play a subsidiary role to the home-based educators (Leask, 2004). Reconfiguring or re-constructing the transnational teaching team (eg Keevers et al, 2019; Leask, 2004) so that local tutors are integral parts of the team can both support the development of professional roles, but also enhance TNE practice more broadly.

Flying faculty teachers

Flying faculty teachers are educators who are based in the degree-awarding institution, but who travel to the partner institution to teach their TNE students. Flying faculty teachers usually engage in intensive, block-teaching sessions, before returning to the home campus, where they might continue to support their students virtually through an online environment and/or be supported by locally based teachers.

My own research has focused on the experiences of flying faculty teachers. During that work, an overview of literature revealed challenges that arise from the role. These include: the physical and environmental impact of long-haul international travel; heavy workloads; potential health risks; and relationships with local tutors (Smith, 2014). One serious threat to TNE is staff burnout. There are also challenges for the local staff as they accommodate the visiting staff and are sometimes required to localise the material they deliver so that it is better understood by the students.

Undoubtedly, flying faculty teaching is hard work – often not the overseas 'jolly' that colleagues not engaged in TNE often believe it to be. Yet, flying faculty teachers also speak of the great benefits that engagement in TNE can bring, particularly in terms of empathy, an expanded worldview and enhanced global appreciation (Smith, 2013), and in job satisfaction, as Example 5.1 shows.

Example 5.1

The importance of interaction with host-country students

Toohey, McGill and Whitsed (2017) carried out a survey of 41 academic staff engaged in TNE. The sample included those who engaged in flying faculty teaching, those who had more extended stays in the host country, and those academics who had no contact with their TNE students as all teaching was carried out by host-country staff. The findings showed that interaction with TNE students, particularly through face-to-face contact during flying faculty and extended visits, was a significant factor in job satisfaction of TNE educators, as it increased the meaningfulness of the work and led to the development of new skills.

While the flying faculty model is more expensive than outsourcing teaching to a partner organisation (McBurnie and Ziguras, 2007, p 54), there can be benefits in terms of job satisfaction and the personal and professional benefits that engagement in the face-to-face teaching of TNE students and the necessary movement into different cultural contexts can bring.

International staff at IBCs

Staff at IBCs are usually based permanently at the offshore campus, rather than visiting there for short trips (L Smith, 2009). While institutions might expect that teaching at IBCs be initially carried out by staff from the home campus through secondments, they cannot rely on secondments alone and can struggle to get academic staff to make a longer-term move to an overseas campus (Salt and Wood, 2014). Staffing at IBCs is often a combination of seconded staff from the home campus (employed by the home university, normally maintaining those terms and conditions, with additional compensatory benefits); international staff (employed by the IBC, with terms and conditions commensurate with the equivalent academic position in the home university); and local staff (recruited locally, with salaries, terms and conditions benchmarked locally) (Healey, 2016), with the proportions of these different groups of staff being a source of tension (Cai and Hall, 2016). There are sometimes challenges in attracting international staff to work at IBCs, and managers recognise the importance of local employment packages in order to recruit and retain talent (Wilkins and Neri, 2019). The differences between the salaries and benefits paid to these different groups can create tensions, and even accusations of discrimination (Healey, 2016).

The need to recruit from a wider international base means that IBCs are not always staffed by people who are familiar with either the educational system of the home campus or an awareness of the host country's culture. This can be challenging in relation to quality assurance, the maintenance of academic standards, and teaching and learning practices. In her study of staff at an Australian IBC in the Middle East, L Smith (2009) found that most of her participants had not been to the Australian campus and had little knowledge of the Australian higher education system. The development and maintenance of the relationship between the IBC and the home campus is therefore key.

It can be equally challenging for staff who move to IBCs from the home institution. Such staff may be familiar with the home campus practices and expect that the IBC will *operate as a microcosm of the home campus transplanted to a new context* (Cai and Hall, 2016, p 218). In their research, Cai and Hall (2016) found that these expatriate staff were challenged to find that there were differences in the routines of work life, which had been underplayed in documentation about the relationship between branch and home campus.

> # Critical questions for practice
>
> » Is your TNE role reflected here? How does it compare?
>
> » How did you find out about the expectations of your role?

Learning, teaching and assessment transnationally

Although educators are not the only group who are involved in TNE, they play a pivotal role in how TNE is practised. There is a growing literature on TNE in relation to learning, teaching and assessment and some of the lessons learnt from that literature will be considered here. I start by looking at curriculum development for TNE, before moving on to its delivery. Chapter 3 introduced the notion of *'packaging curriculum'*, that could be shipped to another context. In addition to the challenges such a transfer has in terms of student experiences, such an approach can impact negatively on practitioners, as it represents *'a disembodiment of the curriculum as the lecturer is thus decentred from the teaching'* (McBurnie and Ziguras, 2007, p 51). I can remember discussing teaching practice with a colleague who taught on a programme with large TNE reach. She had been involved in the curriculum design and was also responsible for its assessment. In our discussion, she referred to Biggs' seminal model of curriculum design, constructive alignment (Biggs, 1996), where intended learning outcomes (ILO), learning and teaching activities, and assessment are aligned to support student learning. My colleague felt frustrated because although she was able to influence the ILOs and the assessment, she had no influence over the learning and teaching activities that her students were engaged in, as these were facilitated by local tutors, with whom she had little interaction. Such disembodiment, she felt, was neither conducive to student learning, nor to her own job satisfaction. This has been noted by other researchers; Toohey et al (2017, p 344) found that *'lack of direct involvement in the delivery of the [TNE] course reduces the responsibility felt for the outcomes of the course'*. Equally, for local tutors, a lack of involvement in curriculum design can reduce feelings of ownership and commitment to the delivery of that curriculum (Waterval et al, 2015, p 76).

Such findings suggest a need for more collegial working between partners in curriculum design and the movements towards more collaborative models of TNE discussed in Chapters 1 and 3. Example 5.1 provides such an example of joint working.

Example 5.2

Merging curricula for a dual degree

Lee (2020) reports on a small-scale study exploring the experiences of four academics (two in China and two in the UK) who worked together to merge Chinese and UK nursing curricula for a dual degree that will run in China. The interviewees reported that it had been a complicated undertaking, where considerable time had been devoted to discussing and understanding the modes of teaching and delivery, assessment tasks, quality outcomes and measurement and better to understand the context. Although time-pressured, complex and a learning curve for all involved, the participants indicated that the process had been beneficial for their development. To support the development and adaptation of curricula that is culturally, socially and professionally appropriate, Lee (2020, p 6) states that *'time for discussion, communication and negotiation, for understanding differences, is crucial for success'*.

In terms of the delivery of learning, teaching and assessment, it could be argued that engaging with TNE students is just like engaging with any international students (and indeed some TNE students will be international students in the host country, as seen in Chapter 2), and that many educators already have experience of teaching a diverse student body in their home-country classrooms. There is an assumption that these international students will adapt (or be supported to adapt) to this new environment. Yet here is where I think the experience of flying faculty can be particularly insightful. In flying faculty TNE experiences, it is not the student that is taken out of their own environment, but the educators. This is articulated well by Crabtree and Sapp (2004), American academics working in Brazil on a postgraduate TNE programme. Their article 'Your Culture, My Classroom, Whose Pedagogy?' challenges the assumptions we make about learning, teaching and assessment and what we expect of our students, and equally what we expect of ourselves. It leads to the question of who adapts and how in relation to learning, teaching and assessment. In the review of literature I carried out to frame research into the professional development potential of flying faculty teachers' experiences (Smith, 2013, pp 127–9), I was able to identify some of the challenges that educators face, and the adaptations they make in response to those challenges. I have summarised these in Table 5.1.

Table 5.1 Themes from the literature on learning, teaching and assessment in flying-faculty mode TNE (summarised from Smith, 2013, pp 127–9).

Theme	Example
Mode of learning	Short and intensive teaching blocks, with the need to deliver curriculum content differently; long teaching days; working through languages other than English and other Englishes.
Relationships	Level of formality in staff–student relationships; hierarchies within classrooms; gender differences and power; classroom environment and interaction; working relationships with local tutors and administrative staff.
Teaching adjustments	Adjustments in response to understandings of time, timeliness and questioning; prior experiences of independent study, criticality and reflection; scaffolding learning through group activities, reinforcement and clear structures.
Learning materials	Adaptation of curriculum for local contexts; the use of local examples, case studies, visits and guest speakers; the impact of adaptation on the 'transnational-ness' of teaching materials.

Some of these are clearly practical and logistical responses to the way in which the TNE is being delivered. There might be, for example, more online elements of a TNE programme and both staff and students may need skill development in order to benefit from working in a virtual environment, or block-teaching models may require a reconfiguring of teaching and learning approaches. In locally delivered models of TNE, staff at the awarding institution may have little or no contact with the students but may well be involved in the marking or moderation of their assessments. It is clearly important that there is good communication between the degree-awarding institution and its TNE partners to ensure that all understand what is expected of assessment, the approaches to marking and the moderation procedures.

In other cases, there are examples of cultural differences in terms of approaches to learning, previous educational experiences and expectations. Support guidance suggests, for example, that TNE students struggle with the development of some generic skills including critical thinking, independent learning, group work, English language, academic integrity and employability (Smith, 2017). We do, however, need to be careful of applying deficit models to TNE students, of seeing them solely through the lens of 'Western' higher education, and labelling their *'deficiencies that need to be fixed and filled up'* (Phan, 2017, p 28). Instead we need to recognise and work with any different experiences and expectations of learning, teaching and assessment and some of the real challenges, often in relation to culture and language, that students can face when engaging in transnational programmes; case study research looking at specific contexts and TNE models can be illuminating (eg Dass, 2019 on franchised provision in TNE; Spencer-Woods, 2019 on Chinese students on articulation degrees).

One way to support the development of learning, teaching and assessment in TNE is to enable more collaborative working within TNE teaching teams. Keay et al (2014) suggest that establishing global communities of practice around TNE could lead to improved teaching and learning. A commitment to joint enterprise, mutual engagement and a shared repertoire can enhance TNE partnership working in ways that are mutually beneficial for partners and students alike. Closer and more collaborative working between transnational colleagues can also, as Leask (2004) has shown, foster intercultural learning and professional development but, like other areas of TNE, requires careful relationship management.

Managing TNE relationships

Much TNE work is about the establishment and management of relationships, and relationships at many different levels. One clear benefit of being involved in TNE is that it can bring you into contact with staff and students from different backgrounds, and this contact can result in the expansion of worldviews and enhanced global appreciation, leading to professional learning and, if supported, potential institutional learning. These relationships are more challenging when working at a distance, when face-to-face time is limited, and/or when there are cultural and linguistic differences. There is a whole plethora of relationships within TNE that need careful management. Three aspects that impact on TNE relationships are explored in more detail here.

Reducing the distance between those engaged in TNE

The importance of geographical distance in TNE should not be downplayed. Partners are frequently located far apart from each other, working in different continents, operating under different time zones.

The widespread use of information and communications technology (ICT) has undoubtedly facilitated the rise of TNE. Indeed, its importance is so great that Wilkinson (2015) asks if technology is *the silent partner in transnational education?'*. Access to enhanced ICT not only facilitates TNE, it can also facilitate the relationships within it. It is now easy to connect people who are geographically dispersed through online conferencing and communication tools, such as Skype, Adobe Connect, or through messaging apps such as WeChat and WhatsApp. This means that meetings can be carried out at a distance, and frequent contact can support the development and maintenance of relationships and contribute to a sense of affiliation. These kinds of tools need good connectivity. Some countries control access to certain apps, webpages and resources and it should not be assumed that all partner institutions will have the technological capacity or capability to engage in this way. Heriot Watt University (HWU), for example, recognised its need for better connectivity when it opened a campus in Malaysia so the new campus could have the same quality of connection as its UK campus (JISC, nd). It worked with the digital and solutions service JISC to enhance its connectivity; one highlighted benefit is that Malaysian students can *'take globally synchronised exams even though they're in different time zones, staff can hold video conferences to discuss the results, and enter them into a single-based student record'* (JISC, nd, p 2).

While such online contact is important and often more practical logistically, there are benefits of face-to-face interaction between partners, in that it physically reduces the geographical distance. Regular visits between TNE partners, exchanges and secondments are all ways in which face-to-face interaction can be supported and distance reduced. Bringing together people, over time, can help build rapport, empathy and understanding necessary to support sustainable relationships.

TNE is practised at a distance; however, not all distance is geographical. The distance between partners can be cultural; equally there can be considerable distance in relation to working conditions and expectations of work.

Working across different cultures

TNE education brings together people who can come from very different backgrounds (educationally, socially, culturally and nationally). These differences can impact on the smooth running of relationships, as misunderstandings can lead to breakdowns in communication. Fielden (2011, p 50) distinguishes between three kinds of cross-cultural differences that can occur in TNE:

1. those relating to personalities;
2. the differences that relate to national characteristics and customs;
3. institutional cultures.

In the first, there might simply be a clash of personalities that means that people are unable to work together. For those leading TNE provision, this might mean finding alternative personnel.

The second can occur where national cultures and the differences between them can impact on TNE relationships. There is a myriad of ways in which national cultures differ, some of which will be visible (eg language, dress, foods), and some will be deeply ingrained (eg concepts of the self, belief systems, familial relationships). These differences are sometimes popularly expressed through the analogy of an iceberg, in which much of what makes up a national culture is hidden beneath the surface of the water (Weaver, 1986). Those engaged in TNE might benefit from professional development in cross-cultural relations, intercultural competence and cultural issues, as the work of Keevers, Lefoe et al (2014, p 241) has shown. Cross-cultural differences can affect how those engaged in TNE relate to and communicate with each other; how learning, teaching and assessment are supported; and how TNE is managed operationally, as Example 5.3 shows.

Example 5.3

The impact of cultural difference on the operational management of TNE

Eldridge and Cranston (2009) interviewed managers responsible for the provision of Australian TNE in Thailand. The sample included participants from the Australian university and the Thai host university. The research, which drew on Hofstede, identified the effects of cultural difference on the academic management of TNE (in terms of pedagogy, assessment and student socialising) and on its operational management (in terms of communication and interaction, and procedures and regulations). Eldridge and Cranston (2009) found that culture differences were evident in how the partners communicated and interacted. A concern for feelings and face meant that Thai colleagues were reluctant to communicate openly and participatory decision making, which was common in the Australian institution, was less successful in Thailand. The perceived (on the Australians' part) lack of direct communication from Thai-based staff also impacted on transparency in relation to administrative procedures. While Hofstede's work and findings from the interviews suggested that the Thais would have a stronger tendency for uncertainty avoidance, the managers felt that the Thais were less concerned about breaking with partnership procedures. The implications for managers were to carefully consider the impact of national cultural differences, which *can be varied and potentially substantial in consequence*' (Eldridge and Cranston, 2009, p 77).

Sometimes the values of the nations in which you are working (or are working with) might be at odds with your own, eg in relation to freedom of speech, human rights and discriminatory practices. This can raise ethical issues for institutions and individuals (see Wilkins, 2017) and may be something that you have to consider carefully.

Finally, differences might be institutional. TNE not only draws together people from different national contexts, but also people situated within different institutional contexts. Institutions have different values and people are influenced by them (Hughes, 2011). Fielden (2011, p 50) reports that different procedures and regulations can create challenges and cause frustration in TNE partnerships. Understanding the partner, their mission, and their motivations for engagement in TNE might help in lessening these differences, combined with more open discussion about the challenges that TNE poses (as Bordogna advocates [2019]).

Power differentials in partnerships

Chapter 3 showed there can be power inequalities in TNE. In addition to power differentials in relation to quality assurance, power can be seen at play in other areas, eg:

» responsibilities and expectations of partners, in terms of decision making and planning (Mwangi, 2017);

» the status of partners (both as institutions and individuals) and the extent to which they are integrated and perceived to be equals (Dobos, 2011; Healey, 2016; Hughes, 2011);

» the tone of the guidance documents that support the partnership (Smith, 2010);

» the different working conditions of staff based at the home campus and those at the IBC (Dobos, 2011; Healey, 2016);

» the privileging of particular forms of (usually Western) knowledge (Mizzi, 2017);

» the role and status of the teacher within the TNE classroom (Smith, 2013).

Some negative impacts of power differentials can be reduced through the development of relationships and communication between partners, a shared commitment to the TNE endeavour, and an understanding of roles and responsibilities. In order to enhance relationships and develop understanding with TNE partners, the University of Greenwich has seconded a member of staff to Malaysia to be the university's link in South East Asia. The success of the role has been recognised by the QAA as good practice (personal communication).

Good leadership of TNE is important (Fielden, 2011); TNE leaders, along with other TNE practitioners, will benefit from professional development.

Critical questions for practice

» What key relationship challenges have you faced in your TNE work?

» What was the source of the challenges: physical distance, culture (personality, national characteristics, institutional) or power inequalities?

Professional development for TNE practice

As indicated in this chapter, and throughout this book, engaging in TNE is a complex practice. It encompasses a wide variety of roles that require different skills and contributes to the expansion and unbundling of the academic, professional and management roles in higher education. TNE calls on practitioners to be adept in managing relationships with people (colleagues and students) with culturally diverse backgrounds and experiences, who are often situated at a distance; to grapple with different approaches to quality assurance, learning, teaching and assessment; to engage in curriculum design and delivery in contexts, or using systems and procedures, that are unfamiliar; and very often to do this where there is no shared first language, and where political, social and ethical values might well be different. There are clearly challenges here. And yet in the face of these challenges, there is often very little targeted support for those who practise transnationally.

New TNE practitioner support

While some new TNE practitioners may benefit from institutional support, many are expected to learn on the job (Hoare, 2013, p 563). This approach can be rife with problems, as Hoare notes (in relation to flying faculty):

The unsupported acculturation during TNE sojourning opens the door to uncomfortable transgression-based learning, high levels of anxiety, the potential to entrench ethnocentrism and, ultimately, to the impoverishment of what could have been a dynamic intercultural learning environment

(2013, p 572)

Another common approach to support those engaged in TNE is through informal mentoring (Gribble and Ziguras, 2003). Here, new TNE practitioners are linked with those who have more experience and this approach is seen as valuable. Yet to rely solely on informal mentoring relations brings its own challenges and rests heavily on the individual mentor and their experiences. If the new TNE practitioner is mentored by someone who has not looked critically and reflectively at their TNE practice, there is a chance that their stereotypes could be reinforced, leading to '*an organisationally entrenched ethnocentrism*', which positions the exporting institution as superior (Hoare, 2013, p 565).

Aside from mentoring, another form of support comes by way of online guides or resources. The example below provides an overview of an online resource for TNE teaching teams (which include degree-awarding and host institution staff).

Example 5.4

Transnational Teaching Teams' online resources

The Transnational Teaching Teams' online resources were developed by the Office for Learning and Teaching in Australia in partnership with universities from Australia, Malaysia and Vietnam. The resources, which were hosted online, included toolkits around different topics pertinent to TNE, such as: inter-cultural group work; participatory action learning for teaching teams; and assessment parity. The resources also included case studies, literature review, research principles and professional development principles (Keevers, Bell et al, 2014, p 4).

As already noted, I authored the Higher Education Academy's (HEA) guide for TNE teachers, the *Transnational Education Toolkit* (Smith, 2017). The principal audience for the *Toolkit* was flying faculty teachers engaged in UK provision. Mizzi (2017, p 249) reviewed materials provided to academics travelling to work in another context temporarily (which includes flying faculty teachers, and those on secondments at IBCs), of which the *Toolkit* would be an example. He found that existing pre-departure information covered topics including living in a new culture, intercultural competency, teaching practices, and local information about transport, recreation facilities and health care. My *Toolkit* contains this kind of information. Although such guidance is useful, it needs to be supplemented with other support.

Courses to support TNE practice development

Some institutions offer a range of credit-bearing and non-credit-bearing courses and programmes to support staff engaged in teaching transnationally, including international collaborative partners (Smith, 2015).

As noted by McBurnie and Ziguras (2007, p 55) many of the issues related to pedagogy for TNE students can be covered through the kinds of educational development opportunities offered by institutions (for example, intercultural communication, or getting to grips with quality assurance); these offerings may also be made available for partner staff through video-conferencing or online programmes. Lamers and Admiral (2018) even recommend that it is worth embedding educational development within the host institution to support the development of teaching. Some universities have developed frameworks to support the professional development of TNE teachers, as the example below shows.

Example 5.5

Professional development framework for TNE teachers

The University of South Australia (UniSA), a pioneer in the development of TNE teachers, won funds from Australian Education International in 2005 to develop a professional development framework for staff teaching Australian programmes transnationally. The framework was developed to reflect three distinct career stages for both academics based in Australia and the local staff at the partner institutions. It set out guidance around the type of content academics might need at each stage and resources included: information pages on UniSA's approach to learning and teaching; induction materials; case study workshops and online workshops. UniSA also developed an online programme called 'Transnational Teaching @ UniSA', which required participants to work through five modules and complete reflective activities and a research report (Hicks and Jarret, 2008).

Professional development for TNE practitioners can come through engagement in existing lecturer development programmes (eg postgraduate certificates in higher education, or equivalent). These courses might be developed, or adapted, for local staff. Alternatively, international partners can join home institution staff on the same programme, as Example 5.6 outlines.

Example 5.6

Lecturer development programmes for TNE partners

The University of Greenwich offers a Postgraduate Certificate in Learning and Teaching in Higher Education that all new lecturers engage in. In 2014–2015, 20 partner staff from Trinidad, who were all teaching on Greenwich programmes, joined the UK-based cohort on this blended programme. The offer of engagement arose following routine contact with the Trinidad partner and the desire to support the development of those partner staff. The Trinidad participants studied alongside the UK participants in a combination of discussion forums and webinars; and online personal tutor group meetings, which complemented the flying faculty visits that Greenwich staff made to Trinidad. The whole cohort benefitted from the intercultural exchange and the approach helped to build teaching and learning communities internationally (Alsford, cited in Smith, 2015).

There can be challenges when providing cross-partner professional development opportunities in terms of who and how they are resourced. Degree-awarding institutions may not have the capacity to provide professional development to the many partners they have dispersed globally (Smith, 2015) and local partners may lack time and resources to engage.

Critical questions for practice

» Who is responsible for the development of TNE practitioners in your institution?

» What (if any) kinds of opportunities are offered?

» Is the approach effective? How could it be improved?

Irrespective of practitioner location, these courses, whether formalised and accredited or informal and one-off, can often lack a focus on the individual and can be disconnected from authentic practice. While some offerings, such as lecturer development programmes, may have strong reflective elements, they relate generally to the development of learning and teaching, and are not specific to the work of TNE practitioners. The development of a critically reflective stance in relation to TNE particularly, with ongoing reflection before, during the TNE work, and when the work is over, is key.

Developing critical reflective practice

Mizzi (2017) outlines a framework for developing a more critically reflective stance towards TNE, which he calls a Pedagogy of Preparedness [PoP]. The PoP involves pre-departure learning of dominant codes, the deconstruction of the TNE teacher and their background, and the decolonising of learning spaces. Attention to these areas may, he argues, *'shift the foreign/local knowledge binary to one of equity and multi-perspective taking'* (Mizzi, 2017, p 257). In my own work on professional development in TNE practice, I have argued strongly for the transformative potential of TNE engagement for flying faculty, particularly when reflection on that engagement is supported following visits (Smith, 2013). Support for reflection can come through conversation-type approaches to practice development which facilitate group reflective discussions (eg Hoare, 2013; Smith, 2017; or more generally Jarvis and Clark, 2020).

In pressured higher education environments, finding the time and space to engage in reflective practice does not always feel possible. One opportunity that might help foster reflection on TNE practice is engagement in schemes which recognise the practice, impact and leadership of learning, teaching and assessment. The UK's AdvanceHE HEA Fellowship is one such scheme, where engagement in and leadership of TNE could provide the evidence of activity, knowledge and values to support recognition across its different categories. Alternatively, such opportunities could be designed into practice-based, multi-site opportunities for collaborative professional learning (Keevers, Lefoe et al, 2014), through collaborative transnational action research projects to develop TNE teaching (Keevers et al, 2019), or through cross-site symposia and conferences.

As has been noted throughout this chapter, there are benefits to working collaboratively and collectively for engagement in TNE to be a rich form of professional learning for TNE practitioners. One approach to collaborative development can come in the form of peer review, as the following example shows.

Example 5.7

Transnational peer review

In an evaluation of a peer review scheme between English teachers working on a partnership programme located in Australia and China, Carolan and Wang (2012) found that process, which used videos and Skype discussions, enabled the teachers to '*build bridges between cultures*', and offered them more '*opportunities to exchange teaching experience, reflect on cross-cultural teaching practices, and develop an integrated pedagogy*' (2012, p 77). The collaborative peer observation was mutually rewarding and was built on a relationship of equality and trust. It allowed the participants to better understand the different contexts in which they worked and to identify development needs.

Such collaborative approaches to professional development can cut across the awarding institution and partner divide, recognising that there is potential to learn from each other. This leads to more equitable, and mutually beneficial learning experiences that benefit TNE practitioners professionally and personally, and which will have knock-on effects for students, and ultimately institutions and the higher education sector more generally.

Summary

- There are many practitioner roles in TNE, but educators have received the most research attention.

- The roles and responsibilities of educators will differ depending on where they are based: at the degree-awarding institution, the host institution or an IBC.

- Flying faculty experiences can provide insight into the challenges of learning, teaching and assessment. More collegial working can help reduce those challenges.

- Relationship management in TNE is difficult due to physical distance, cultural differences and power differentials.

- Due to the complexity of TNE, professional development opportunities should be available for TNE practitioners so they can learn and develop from their experiences.

Useful texts

Dunn, L and Wallace, M (eds) (2008) *Teaching in Transnational Higher Education: Enhancing Learning for Offshore International Students.* Abingdon: Routledge.

Lee Dunn and Michelle Wallace's edited collection on Teaching in Transnational Higher Education *contains useful chapters on a range of topics including intercultural dialogue, plagiarism and reflective practice.*

Smith, K (2013) Overseas Flying Faculty Teaching as a Trigger for Transformative Professional Development. *International Journal for Academic Development*, 18: 127–38.

My article on transformative professional development also contains a literature review on the learning, teaching and assessment challenges that flying faculty teachers face (which were summarised in this chapter).

In this chapter, I reflect on what inspired me to write this book, the journey it has taken us on and, finally, I share some thoughts on the future of TNE.

Where did it begin?

This is not a foray into the history of TNE but rather a reflection on my own interest in the area and how this has shaped this book. In 2006, I was a flying faculty teacher on a UK top-up social science degree programme in Hong Kong. I travelled to Hong Kong three times a year and worked with students on week-long intensive courses. When I was in the UK, my students were supported through seminars with Hong Kong-based tutors. Alongside my teaching on this programme, I was an educational developer, working in a central department. I noted that there was very little support or guidance for TNE practitioners. This was the beginning of my research and practice-development interest in TNE. My research has focused on professional development for flying faculty (K Smith, 2009, 2013, 2015), on their expectations, experiences and motivations (Smith, 2014) and on national policy and guidance for TNE (Smith, 2010). I went on to author the *Transnational Education Toolkit* (Smith, 2017) for the Higher Education Academy (now AdvanceHE), which drew together resources and research to provide a practical guide for those delivering UK degree awards transnationally. All this previous work has a strong focus on flying faculty and the specific challenges and opportunities that this form of TNE brings.

My further engagement in TNE has led me to discover the many forms of TNE, offered in different modes, configurations and reflecting different relationships between higher education providers. Through this book, I hope to have introduced you to some of this diversity in an accessible manner. If you are already involved in TNE, you may feel that your own views, like mine, have been framed by your experiences; this book may have widened your understanding of TNE and how it is practised. Drawing on a wide range of TNE-focused research, raising critical issues and asking critical questions for practice, I hope I have inspired you to think critically about your own, your institution's and your nation's engagement in TNE, and how TNE has been and is being driven globally. While I have aimed to reflect the diversity of TNE through the materials I have chosen, I also recognise my own positioning and experiences that will inevitably have shaped the approach that I have adopted. I sit within the Global North and have practitioner and research experience of the export of education from the North to the South and East. Colleagues with different backgrounds, experiences and geographical locations may perceive TNE differently, and I hope that this book provides a provocation to reflect on those TNE practices.

Where have we been?

Throughout the book, the complexity of TNE has been indicated. While this can be challenging for researchers and practitioners alike, it is also what makes TNE such an interesting area to engage in.

Chapter 1 introduced the concept of TNE and how it fits within internationalisation agendas. It quickly became apparent that TNE is a catch-all term, used to describe many different approaches to education where students are located in a different country to where the degree-awarding institution is based, with different underlying models (broadly distance education, local partner delivery models, and physical presence) and different foundations for the relationships between partners. This chapter showed how TNE has evolved and will continue to evolve in response to changing environments and priorities. The key message from this chapter is not to assume that when you talk to someone about TNE you will be talking about the same thing. It is worth clarifying with them what TNE means to you within your own context.

Chapter 2 discussed motivations for engagement in TNE, focusing on global drivers and how they play out nationally, institutionally and for individual practitioners. Like the definitions of TNE, the motivations for engagement are equally diverse and multifarious. These motivations also change and evolve, based on the experience and experiences of those involved – some of these drivers may be stronger than others at different times and in different places, and reflect the prevailing view of TNE (eg as a 'commercial' or a 'community' endeavour [Becker, 2018]). There is merit in critically exploring the drivers for your institution's engagement in TNE and the extent to which they align with your own.

Chapter 3 took quality assurance as its focus. For many practitioners, quality plays a significant role in their engagement with TNE and can be the source of frustration due to the roles that people need to play. The chapter outlined why questions of quality are so key in TNE and showed how quality assurance is guided globally and nationally, and then played out institutionally. The complexity of TNE was once again highlighted in relation, particularly, to notions of equivalence. Research and practitioner experiences of quality assurance in TNE suggest that more collaborative approaches can be effective in both assuring and enhancing the quality of TNE. You may want to think about your own experiences of quality assurance and how responsibilities are managed and shared.

Chapter 4 explored TNE students and their experiences. An initial challenge was raised in relation to understanding the student experience in that accurate records regarding TNE students are not always available; countries, if they do collect TNE student data at all, do not always count the same things. The discussion of student motivations to engage in TNE also surfaced the challenges of seeing TNE as a binary choice between 'home' and 'abroad' education, with TNE students also now choosing to be international students in a TNE host country, which both complicates and colours TNE practice further. The chapter raised questions about TNE student affiliation and association with the institutions who deliver the education, those who supply it, and with the countries where the education is provided and from whence it originated. With such diversity of experience and background, it is not possible to talk about 'the TNE student experience', though this chapter did explore TNE learning environments and learning opportunities. There is clearly space for more research into TNE students' experiences, and you might want to reflect on what you already know about your TNE students (if you have them), what it would be useful to know, and how you would find out.

Finally, Chapter 5 concentrated on TNE practitioners. You might be a TNE practitioner yourself and the initial list of roles showed that there are many ways that people can be engaged in TNE within current higher education. The chapter looked specifically at three educator roles and showed some of the differences between them, which resulted, primarily, from institutional positioning, and learning, teaching and assessment were explored specifically. Managing the relationships between TNE practitioners is important and can be made more difficult due to the physical distances involved, national differences and power differentials. Engaging in TNE is challenging and opportunities for professional development should be available for all practitioners. It is my hope that this book contributes to your own professional learning and development, and that you are inspired to seek out the readings and resources that I have referenced to further develop your knowledge and understanding of the areas of TNE that interest you most.

In an area as broad, diverse and complicated as TNE, and in a book of this brevity, it would not be possible to cover all permutations of TNE from all perspectives. Instead, I have provided an introduction that covers some critical questions about current TNE for you to consider. In the final section, I will conclude with some brief reflections on where TNE might be heading.

Where are we going?

In many respects, it is difficult to predict the future of TNE, as it is responsive to market demands and policy change. The rise of TNE has been rapid, with relatively more developed higher education systems or those with excess capacity responding to the requests from countries who felt they could benefit from the provision of education from elsewhere. Will this strongly commercial and export-driven approach to TNE continue? Some commentators believe that TNE has had its time. Healey (2019), writing specifically about the UK which historically has been one of the leading exporters of higher education, notes that many of the drivers for the UK's engagement in TNE have weakened, that the UK is more aware of the risks (financial and reputational) of engaging in TNE partnerships, and that host governments are more confident in their ability to provide the education their country needs. Healey (2019) argues that while TNE is not over, it is *'the beginning of the end'* (Healey 2019, p 9).

I am less inclined to project its demise, yet I recognise that TNE will change. Fuelled by technological, societal, economic, political and environmental drivers, TNE will evolve and adapt to the different circumstances in which it finds itself. We already see indications of that now.

Developments in technology and the ability to engage in synchronous online delivery means that the physical location of students and TNE providers is becoming increasingly irrelevant (Lawton and Tsiligiris, 2018) and students will be able to access high-quality higher education wherever they are in the world (WECD/UUKi, 2018). Increased use of technologically enhanced support (if available universally) could contribute to mitigating the global climate crisis by signalling an end to the long-haul visits by aeroplane that epitomise flying faculty models of TNE. At the same time, the distinction between 'home' and 'abroad' provision is becoming more and more blurred with institutions defining themselves as 'global universities' which enable seamless transfer between (transnational) sites (Lawton and Tsiligiris, 2018) and also a shift from transnational to multinational education, where *'managerial decision-making processes and stakeholder interests'* are multinational (Healey and Bordogna, 2014, p 51).

There are also changes in the relationships between those who have traditionally imported transnational education and those countries that have predominantly exported, and new players are entering the TNE market and changing the flow of education, which had been traditionally Global North to South (eg the establishment of Bucheon University, South Korea; in Tashkent, Uzbekistan [Chung, 2019]) and engaging in different kinds of partnership arrangement. With the maturation of their higher education systems, some traditional importers are no longer looking to import anything; TNE becomes part of a wider strategy for internationalisation through partnership (Lawton and Tsiligiris, 2019). Commentators suggest the shift towards more collaborative models of TNE will continue, focusing on deeper and more equitable and bi-directional partnerships through dual and joint degrees and international universities (Knight, 2017; Lawton and Tsiligiris, 2018). As someone who has long argued, through my own research, for the emphasis to be placed on collaboration, shared responsibility and the mutual benefits of engagement in the practice of TNE, I welcome these movements.

Despite (or perhaps because of) its complexity and challenge, TNE is an exciting area of higher education to work in. If you have not had that experience yet, I hope this book has whetted your appetite. If you are already a TNE practitioner, I hope that it has led you to think critically about the ways in which you engage transnationally and why.

Useful texts

Healey, N M (2019) The End of Transnational Education? The View from the UK. *Perspectives: Policy and Practice in Higher Education*. [online] Available at: www.tandfonline.com/doi/abs/10.1080/13603108.2019.1631227?journalCode=t psp20 (accessed 16 January 2020).

Nigel Healey's article predicts the decline of TNE in the UK due to changes in the forces that fuelled its initial growth.

Lawton, T and Tsiligiris, V (2018) The Future of TNE. In Tsiligiris, V and Lawton, W (eds), *Exporting Transnational Education*, (pp 217–26). Cham: Palgrave Macmillan.

William Lawton and Vangelis Tsiligiris outline their view of the future of TNE in the final chapter of their collection of essays on the export of TNE.

References

Ahmad, S Z and Buchanan, F R (2016) Choices of Destination for Transnational Higher Education: "Pull" Factors in an Asia Pacific Market. *Educational Studies*, 42: 163–80.

Akram, A, Merunka, D and Shakaib Akram, M (2011) Perceived Brand Globalness in Emerging Markets and the Moderating Role of Consumer Ethnocentrism. *International Journal of Emerging Markets*, 6: 291–303.

Arunasalam, N (2016) Malaysian Nurses' Motivation to Study on Transnational Higher Education Programmes. *The Malaysian Journal of Nursing*, 7: 34–41.

Ashour, S (2018) Branding of Germany's Transnational Education and Its Potentials in the Arabian Gulf Region. *Cogent Education*, 5. [online] Available at: www.tandfonline.com/doi/full/10.1080/2331186X.2018.1463936 (accessed 16 January 2020).

Becker, R (2018) Shaping Transnational Education in the Netherlands: National Policy Directions. In Tsiligiris, V and Lawton, W (eds) *Exporting Transnational Education* (pp 27–44). Cham: Palgrave Macmillan.

BBC (2015) "Twin" Robin Hood Statue Given to China, *BBC News*, 1 August 2015. [online] Available at: www.bbc.co.uk/news/uk-england-nottinghamshire-33732613 (accessed 16 January 2020).

Biggs, J (1996) Enhancing Teaching Through Constructive Alignment. *Higher Education*, 32: 347–64.

BIS (2014) *The Value of Transnational Education to the UK*. London: Department for Innovation and Skills. [online] Available at: https://assets.publishing.service.gov.uk/government/uploads/system/uploads/attachment_data/file/387910/bis-14-1202-the-value-of-transnational-education-to-the-uk.pdf (accessed 16 January 2020).

Blackmur, D (2007) A Critical Analysis of the UNESCO/OECD Guidelines for Quality Provision of Cross-Border Higher Education. *Quality in Higher Education*, 13: 117–30.

Bodycott, P and Walker, A (2000) Teaching Abroad: Lessons Learned about Inter-Cultural Understanding for Teachers in Higher Education. *Teaching in Higher Education*, 5: 79–94.

Bordogna, C M (2019) Are Degree-Awarding Institutions Doing Enough to Support the Implementation of Quality Assurance in Transnational Higher Education Partnerships? *Journal of Studies in International Education*. [online] Available at: https://journals.sagepub.com/doi/abs/10.1177/1028315319888458 (accessed 16 January 2020).

Bothwell, E (2019) Reading 'Ignored Warning Signals' over Malaysia Branch Campus. *Times Higher Education*, 2 January. [online] Available at: www.timeshighereducation.com/news/reading-ignored-warning-signals-over-malaysia-branch-campus (accessed 16 January 2020).

British Council (2012a) *The Shape of Things to Come: Higher Education Global Trends and Emerging Opportunities to 2020*. [online] Available at: www.britishcouncil.org/sites/default/files/the_shape_of_things_to_come_-_higher_education_global_trends_and_emerging_opportunities_to_2020.pdf (accessed 16 January 2020).

British Council (2012b) *Portrait of a Transnational Education Student*. London: British Council, Education Intelligence.

British Council (2013) *The Shape of Things to Come: The Evolution of Transnational Education: Data, Definitions, Opportunities and Impacts Analysis*. [online] Available at: www.britishcouncil.org/sites/default/files/the_shape_of_things_to_come_2.pdf (accessed 16 January 2020).

Cai, L and Hall, C (2016) Motivations, Expectations, and Experiences of Expatriate Academic Staff on an International Branch Campus in China. *Journal of Studies in International Education*, 20: 207–22.

Campbell, C and van der Wende, M (2000) *International Initiatives and Trends in Quality Assurance for European Higher Education*. Helsinki: The European Network for Quality Assurance in Higher Education.

Carolan, L and Wang, L (2012) Reflections on a Transnational Peer Review of Teaching. *ELT Journal*, 66: 71–80.

Chee, C M, Mohsin Butt, M, Wilkins, S and Ong, F S (2016) Country of Origin and Country of Service Delivery Effects in Transnational Higher Education: A Comparison of International Branch Campuses from Developed and Developing Nations. *Journal for Marketing for Higher Education*, 26: 86–102.

Choudaha, R and Edelstein, R J (2014) Towards Quality Transnational Education. *University World News*, 15 October. [online] Available at: www.universityworldnews.com/post.php?story=20141015210003860 (accessed 16 January 2020).

Chung, A (2019) Universities to Get Go-Ahead to Set Up Campuses Abroad. *University World News*, 26 September. [online] Available at: www.universityworldnews.com/post.php?story=20190926135137687 (accessed 16 January 2020).

Clarke, A, Johal, T, Sharp, K and Quinn, S (2016) Achieving Equivalence: A Transnational Curriculum Design Framework. *International Journal for Academic Development*, 21: 364–76.

Coleman, D (2003) Quality Assurance in Transnational Education. *Journal of Studies in International Education*, 7: 354–78.

Crabtree, R D and Sapp, D A (2004) Your Culture, My Classroom, Whose Pedagogy? Negotiating Effective Teaching and Learning in Brazil. *Journal of Studies in International Education*, 8: 105–32.

Dai, K and Garcia, J (2019) Intercultural Learning in Transnational Articulation Programs: The Hidden Agenda of Chinese Students' Experiences. *Journal of International Students*, 9: 362–83.

Dass, R (2019) *Perceptions of UK Franchised TNE in Vietnam, and Its Impact on Curriculum Innovation*. Unpublished EdD thesis, University of Greenwich.

Debowski, S (2005) Across the Divide: Teaching a Transnational MBA in a Second Language. *Higher Education Research and Development*, 24: 265–80.

De Montfort University (DMU) (nd) *Strategic Plan 2018–2023*. [online] Available at: www.dmu.ac.uk/documents/university-governance/strategic-plan-2018–23.pdf (accessed 16 January 2020).

Department of Education and Training (2018) *Offshore Delivery of Australian Higher Education Courses in 2017*. [online] Available at: https://internationaleducation.gov.au/research/Research-Snapshots/Documents/RS_Offshore%20HE_2017.pdf (accessed 16 January 2020).

Department for International Trade (DIT) (2015) *Exporting is GREAT – Major Opportunities Programme Launches*. [online] Available at: www.gov.uk/government/news/exporting-is-great-major-opportunities-programme-launches (accessed 16 January 2020).

Department for International Trade (DIT) (2017) *Department for International Trade Announces New Initiatives to Support UK Education Exports*. [online] Available at: www.gov.uk/government/news/department-for-international-trade-announces-new-initiatives-to-support-uk-education-exports (accessed 16 January 2020).

Department for International Trade (DIT) (2019) *UK Revenue from Education Related Exports and Transnational Education Activity in 2016*. [online] Available at: https://assets.publishing.service.gov.uk/government/uploads/system/uploads/attachment_data/file/773167/SFR_Education_Exports_2016.pdf (accessed 16 January 2020).

De Wit, H (2002) *Internationalisation of Higher Education in the United States of America and Europe: A Historical, Comparative, and Conceptual Analysis*. Westport, CT: Greenwood Press.

Dobos, K (2011) 'Serving Two Masters' – Academics' Perspectives on Working at an Offshore Campus. *Educational Review*, 63: 19–35.

Doorbar, A and Bateman, C (2008) The Growth of Transnational Higher Education: The UK Perspective. In Dunn, L and Wallace, M (eds) *Teaching in Transnational Education: Enhancing Learning for Offshore International Students* (pp. 14–22). London: Routledge.

Dunn, L and Wallace, M (2008) *Teaching in Transnational Higher Education*. London: Routledge.

Edwards, J, Crosling, G and Edwards, R (2010) Outsourcing University Degrees: Implications for Quality Control. *Journal of Higher Education Policy and Management*, 32: 303–15.

Eldridge, K and Cranston, N (2009) Managing Transnational Education: Does National Culture Really Matter? *Higher Education Policy and Management*, 31: 67–79.

Fang, W and Wang, S (2014) Chinese Students' Choice of Transnational Higher Education in a Globalized Higher Education Market: A Case Study of W University. *Journal of Studies in International Education*, 18: 475–94.

Fielden, J (2011) *Leadership and Management in International Partnerships*. London: Leadership Foundation. [online] Available at: www.lfhe.ac.uk/en/research-resources/research-hub/2011-research/leadership-and-management-of-international-partnerships.cfm (accessed 16 January 2020).

Fielden, J (2013) *A Guide to the Financial Aspects of UK HEI Offshore Activities*. London: UK Higher Education International Unit. [online] Available at: www.universitiesuk.ac.uk/policy-and-analysis/reports/Documents/International/OffshoreFinancingFINALMarch13.pdf (accessed 16 January 2020).

Gribble, K and Ziguras, C (2003) Learning to Teach Offshore: Pre-Departure Training for Lecturers in Transnational Programs. *Higher Education Research and Development*, 22: 205–16.

Harvey, L and Green, D (1993) Defining Quality. *Assessment and Evaluation in Higher Education*, 18: 9–34.

Havergal, C (2018) Lancaster Mulls European Branch Campus Post-Brexit. *Times Higher Education*, 24 July. [online] Available at: www.timeshighereducation.com/news/lancaster-mulls-european-branch-campus-post-brexit (accessed 16 January 2020).

Healey, N (2013) Is UK Transnational Education 'One of Britain's Great Growth Industries of the Future'? *Higher Education Review*, 45: 6–35.

Healey, N M (2015) Towards a Risk-Based Typology for Transnational Education. *Higher Education*, 69: 1–18.

Healey, N M (2016) The Challenges of Leading an International Branch Campus: The 'Lived Experience' of In-Country Senior Managers. *Journal of Studies in International Education*, 20: 61–78.

Healey, N M (2019) The End of Transnational Education? The View from the UK. *Perspectives: Policy and Practice in Higher Education*. [online] Available at: www.tandfonline.com/doi/abs/10.1080/13603108.2019.1631227?journalCode=tpsp20 (accessed 16 January 2020).

Healey, N M and Bordogna, C (2014) From Transnational to Multinational Education: Emerging Trends in International Higher Education. *Internationalisation of Higher Education*, 3: 33–56.

HEFCE (2014) *Directions of Travel: Transnational Pathways into UK Higher Education*. [online] Available at: https://dera.ioe.ac.uk/23144/1/HEFCE2015_08.pdf (accessed 16 January 2020).

HEGlobal (2016) *The Scale and Scope of UK Higher Education – Transnational Education*. London: UK HE International Unit.

HESA (2016) *Aggregate Offshore Record 2016/17 – Introduction*. [online] Available at: www.hesa.ac.uk/collection/c16052/introduction (accessed 16 January 2020).

Hicks, M and Jarrett, K (2008) Providing Instructions, Orientation and Professional Development for All Staff Involved in Transnational Teaching. In Dunn, L and Wallace, M (eds) *Teaching in Transnational Higher Education* (pp. 238–48). London: Routledge.

Hill, C, Cheong, K-C, Leong, Y-C and Fernandez-Chung, R (2014) TNE – Transnational Education or Tensions Between National and External? A Case Study of Malaysia. *Studies in Higher Education*, 39: 952–66.

Hoare, L (2012) Transnational Student Voices: Reflections on a Second Chance. *Journal of Studies in International Education*, 16: 271–86.

Hoare, L (2013) Swimming in the Deep End: Transnational Teaching as Culture Learning? *Higher Education Research & Development*, 32: 561–74.

Hou, J, Montgomery, C and McDowell, L (2014) Exploring the Diverse Motivations of Transnational Higher Education in China: Complexities and Contradictions. *Journal of Education for Teaching*, 40: 300–18.

Hughes, R (2011) Strategies for Managing and Leading an Academic Staff in Multiple Countries. *New Directions for Higher Education*, 155: 19–28.

Inge, S (2018) Expansion of UK Transnational Education Provision Tails Off. *Times Higher Education*, 2 February. [online] Available at: www.timeshighereducation.com/news/expansion-uk-transnational-education-provision-tails (accessed 16 January 2020).

Jarvis, J and Clark, K (2020) *Conversations to Change Teaching*. St Albans: Critical Publishing.

JISC (nd) *Case Study: Enabling Global Working at a Global University*. [online] Available at: http://repository.jisc.ac.uk/6692/1/TNE_Case_Study_Heriot_Watt.pdf (accessed 16 January 2020).

Jo, H-R (2017) Incheon Global Campus at Forefront of Education in Northeast. *The Korea Herald*, 15 December. [online] Available at: http://www.koreaherald.com/view.php?ud=20171214000971 (accessed 16 January 2020).

Kane, T (2014) Whose Lingua Franca? The Politics of Language in Transnational Medical Education. *The Journal of General Education*, 63: 94–112.

Keay, J, May, H and O' Mahony, J (2014) Improving Learning and Teaching in Transnational Education: Can Communities of Practice Help? *Journal of Education for Teaching*, 40: 251–66.

Keevers, L M, Price, O, Leask, B, Dawood Sultan, F K P and Lim, J S Y (2019) Practices to Improve Collaboration by Reconfiguring Boundaries in Transnational Education. *Journal of University Teaching & Learning Practice*, 16: 1–15.

Keevers, L, Bell, M, Ganesharatnam, S, Dawood Sultan, F K P, See Yin Lim, J, Loh, V, Lefoe, G, Hall, C and Scholz, C (2014) *Transnational Teaching Teams: Professional Development for Quality Enhancement of Teaching and Learning-Final Report*. Sydney: Office for Learning and Teaching. [online] Available at: https://pdfs.semanticscholar.org/43a4/dad77e15513c268dfde582b06ad5ba84c3b7.pdf (accessed 16 January 2020).

Keevers, L, Lefoe, G, Leask, B, Sultan, F K, Ganesharatnam, S, Loh, V and Lim, J (2014) 'I Like the People I Work With. Maybe I'll Get to Meet Them in Person One Day': Teaching and Learning Practice Development with Transnational Teaching Teams. *Journal of Education for Teaching: International Research and Pedagogy*, 40: 232–50.

Kemp, N (2018) UK TNE Delivery and the Role of Partners. Paper presented at the *Raising Standards of Transnational Higher Education* Inside Government event, 13 December, London.

Kennedy, K (2019) UK Home Secretary Calls for Post-Study Work Restrictions to be Lifted. *The Pie News*, 10 June. [online] Available at: https://thepienews.com/news/uk-home-secretary-calls-for-a-lifting-of-psw-restrictions-on-international-students (accessed 16 January 2020).

Kim, T (2010) Transnational Academic Mobility, Knowledge, and Identity Capital. *Discourse: Studies in the Cultural Politics of Higher Education*, 31: 577–91.

Knight, J (2003) Updated Internationalization Definition. *International Higher Education*, 33: 2–3.

Knight, J (2005) *Borderless, Offshore, Transnational and Cross-Border Education: Definition and Data Dilemmas*. London: OBHE.

Knight, J (2016) Transnational Education Remodeled: Toward a Common TNE Framework and Definitions. *Journal of Studies in International Education*, 20: 34–47.

Knight, J (2017) The New Faces of Transnational Higher Education. *University World News*, 27 October. [online] Available at: www.universityworldnews.com/article.php?story=20171024133538586 (accessed 16 January 2020).

Knight, J and Liu, Q (2016) Crossborder and Transnational Higher Education. *Oxford Bibliographies*. [online] Available at: www.oxfordbibliographies.com/view/document/obo-9780199756810/obo-9780199756810-0176.xml (accessed 16 January 2020).

Knight, J and McNamara, J (2017) *Transnational Education: A Classification Framework and Data Collection Guidelines for International Programme and Provider Mobility (IPPM)*. [online] Available at: www.britishcouncil.org/sites/default/files/tne_classification_framework-final.pdf (accessed 16 January 2020).

Kosmützky, A and Putty, R (2015) Transcending Border and Traversing Boundaries: A Systematic Review of the Literature on Transnational, Offshore, Cross-Border, and Borderless Higher Education. *Journal of Studies in International Education*, 20: 8–33.

Lamers, A M and Admirall, W F (2018) Moving Out of Their Comfort Zones: Enhancing Teaching Practice in Transnational Education. *International Journal for Academic Development*, 23: 110–22.

Lamers-Reeuwijk, A M, Admiraal, W F and van der Rijst, R M (2019) Expatriate Academic and Transnational Teaching: The Need for Quality Assurance and Quality Enhancement to Go Hand in Hand. *Higher Education Research and Development*. [online] Available at: www.tandfonline.com/doi/full/10.1080/07294360.2019.1693516 (accessed 16 January 2020).

Lane, J E and Kinser, K (2012) International Branch Campuses: One Definition to Rule Them All? *The Chronicle of Higher Education*, 18 January. [online] Available at: www.chronicle.com/blogs/worldwise/international-branch-campuses-one-definition-to-rule-them-all/29051 (accessed 16 January 2020).

Lawton, T and Tsiligiris, V (2018) The Future of TNE. In Tsiligiris, V and Lawton, W (eds) *Exporting Transnational Education* (pp 217–26). Cham: Palgrave Macmillan.

Leask, B (2004) *Transnational Education and Intercultural Learning: Reconstructing the Offshore Teaching Team to Enhance Internationalisation*. Proceedings of the Australian Universities Quality Forum. [online] Available at: http://citeseerx.ist.psu.edu/viewdoc/download?doi=10.1.1.114.9090&rep=rep1&type=pdf (accessed 16 January 2020).

Lee, A (2020) An (Interpretive) Phenomenological Analysis of Nursing Professionals Experience of Developing a Transnational Curriculum. *Nurse Education Today*, 84. [online] Available at: www.sciencedirect.com/science/article/pii/S0260691719302552 (accessed 16 January 2020).

Levatino, A (2015) Transnational Higher Education and Skilled Migration: Evidence from Australia. *International Journal of Educational Development*, 40: 106–16.

Lim, C B, Bentley, D, Henderson, F, Pan, S Y, Balakrishan, V D, Balasingam, D M and Teh, Y Y (2016) Equivalent or Not? Beyond Measuring Teaching and Learning Standards in a Transnational Education Environment. *Quality Assurance in Education*, 24: 528–40.

Lim, F C B (2010) Do Too Many Rights Make a Wrong? A Qualitative Study of the Experiences of a Sample of Malaysian and Singapore Private Higher Education Providers in Transnational Quality Assurance. *Quality in Higher Education*, 16: 211–22.

Magne, P, Poverjuc, O and Heffernan, T (2017) Pedagogies Across Borders: Perspectives from Teaching Staff and Students Engaged with Transnational Programmes in Hong Kong. *Practice and Evidence of Scholarship of Teaching and Learning in Higher Education*, 12: 45–62.

Marginson, S and van der Wende, M (2007) Globalisation and Higher Education. *OECD Education Working Papers*. Paris: OECD Publishing. [online] Available at: http://dx.doi.org/10.1787/173831738240 (accessed 16 January 2020).

Mazzarol, T and Soutar, G N (2002) 'Push-Pull' Factors Influencing International Student Destination Choice. *The International Journal of Educational Management*, 16: 82–90.

McBurnie, G and Ziguras, C (2007) *Transnational Education: Issues and Trends in Offshore Higher Education*. Abingdon: Routledge.

McNamara, J and Knight, J (2015) *Transnational Education Data Collection Systems: Awareness, Analysis, Action*. [online] Available at: www2.daad.de/medien/hochschulen/projekte/studienangebote/2015_tnb_study_daad-bc_2_data_collection.pdf (accessed 16 January 2020).

Mellors-Bourne, R (2017) *The Wider Benefits of Transnational Education to the UK*. [online] Available at: https://assets.publishing.service.gov.uk/government/uploads/system/uploads/attachment_data/file/624364/CRAC_TNE_report_final.pdf (accessed 16 January 2020).

Mellors-Bourne, R, Jones, E and Woodfield, R (2015) *Transnational Education and Employability Development*. York: Higher Education Academy. [online] Available at: www.heacademy.ac.uk/knowledge-hub/transnational-education-and-employability-development (accessed 16 January 2020).

Mellors-Bourne, R, Fielden, J, Kemp, N, Middlehurst, R and Woodfield, S (2014) *The Value of Transnational Education to the UK.* [online] Available at: https://assets.publishing.service.gov.uk/government/uploads/system/uploads/attachment_data/file/387910/bis-14-1202-the-value-of-transnational-education-to-the-uk.pdf (accessed 16 January 2020).

Miller, N (2013) *Strategic Affinity: Engaging International Alumni to Support Internationalisation.* York: Higher Education Academy. [online] Available at: www.advance-he.ac.uk/knowledge-hub/strategic-affinity-engaging-international-alumni-support-internationalisation (accessed 16 January 2020).

Mitchell, N (2018) TNE Could Widen Access to World's Poorest Communities. *University World News,* 18 January. [online] Available at: www.universityworldnews.com/post.php?story=20180118201602386 (accessed 16 January 2020).

Mizzi, R C (2017) Bridging Borders: Toward a Pedagogy of Preparedness for Visiting Faculty. *Journal of Studies in International Education,* 21: 246–60.

Mok, H K and Han, X (2016) From 'Brain Drain' to 'Brain Bridging': Transnational Higher Education Development and Graduate Employment in China. *Journal of Higher Education Policy and Management,* 38: 369–89.

Montgomery, C (2016) Transnational Partnerships in Higher Education in China: The Diversity and Complexity of Elite Strategic Alliances. *London Review of Education,* 14: 70–85.

Mwangi, C A G (2017) Partner Positioning: Examining International Higher Education Partnerships Through a Mutuality Lens. *The Review of Higher Education,* 41: 33–60.

Nahn, T T and Nguyen, H C (2018) Quality Challenges in Transnational Higher Education under Profit-Driven Motives: The Vietnamese Experience. *Issues in Educational Research,* 28: 138–52.

Naidoo, V (2009) Transnational Higher Education: A Stock Take of Current Activity. *Journal of Studies in International Education,* 13: 310–30.

Nida, E A and Taber, C R (1974) *The Theory and Practice of Translation.* Leiden: E J Brill.

O'Callaghan, C (2017) *Transnational Education: Navigating Regulation and Innovation in Overseas Distance Learning.* [online] Available at: https://ahua.ac.uk/challenges-overseas-higher-education-regulation-distance-learning (accessed 16 January 2020).

O'Carroll, L (2018) Bring Back Work Visas for Overseas Graduates, Say UK Universities. *The Guardian,* 4 September. [online] Available at: www.theguardian.com/education/2018/sep/04/bring-back-work-visas-overseas-graduates-say-uk-universities (accessed 16 January 2020).

O'Keeffe, P (2013) A Sense of Belonging: Improving Student Retention. *College Student Journal,* 47: 605–13.

O'Mahony, J (2014) *Enhancing Student Learning and Teacher Development in Transnational Education.* York: Higher Education Academy. [online] Available at: www.advance-he.ac.uk/knowledge-hub/enhancing-student-learning-and-teacher-development-transnational-education (accessed 16 January 2020).

OECD (2005) *Guidelines for Quality Provision in Cross-border Higher Education.* Paris: OECD. [online] Available at: www.oecd.org/education/skills-beyond-school/35779480.pdf (accessed 16 January 2020).

Pells, R (2019) UK Campus Will Teach China to Open Education to World, Says Dean. *Times Higher Education,* 22 June. [online] Available at: www.timeshighereducation.com/news/uk-campus-will-teach-china-open-education-world-says-dean (accessed 16 January 2020).

Phan, L H (2017) *Transnational Education Crossing 'Asia' and 'the West'. Adjusted Desire, Transformative Mediocrity, Neo-Colonial Desire.* London: Routledge.

Pyvis, D and Chapman, A (2005) Identity and Social Practice in Higher Education: Student Experiences of Postgraduate Courses Delivered 'Offshore' in Singapore and Hong Kong by an Australian University. *International Journal of Educational Development,* 25: 39–52.

Pyvis, D and Chapman, A (2007) Why University Students Choose an International Education: A Case Study in Malaysia. *International Journal of Educational Development,* 27: 235–46.

QAA (2014) *Review of UK Transnational Education in United Arab Emirates: Overview.* [online] Available at: www.qaa.ac.uk/docs/qaa/international/review-transnational-education-uae-14.pdf?sfvrsn=1407f481_2%20%E2%80%93# (accessed 16 January 2020).

QAA (2017) *Country Report: The United Arab Emirates.* [online] Available at: www.qaa.ac.uk/docs/qaa/international/country-report-uae-2017.pdf?sfvrsn=25caf781_6 (accessed 16 January 2020).

QAA (2018a) *Enhancing the UK TNE Student Experience in Dubai and Singapore: A Case Study of Cross-Border Cooperation.* [online] Available at: www.qaa.ac.uk/docs/qaa/international/enhancing-the-uk-tne-student-experience-in-dubai-and-singapore.pdf (accessed 16 January 2020).

QAA (2018b) *The Right to Award UK Degrees.* [online] Available at: www.qaa.ac.uk/docs/qaa/guidance/the-right-to-award-degrees-18.pdf?sfvrsn=4a2f781_14 (accessed 16 March 2020).

Salt, J and Wood, P (2014) Staffing UK University Campuses Overseas: Lessons from MNE Practice. *Journal of Studies in International Education*, 18: 82–97.

Schindler, L, Puls-Elvidge, S, Welzant, H and Crawford, L (2015) Definitions of Quality in Higher Education: A Synthesis of the Literature. *Higher Learning Research Communications*, 5: 3–13.

Sharp, K (2017) The Distinction between Academic Standards and Quality: Implications for Transnational Higher Education. *Quality in Higher Education*, 23: 138–52.

Siltaoja, M, Juusola, K and Kivijärvi, M (2019) 'World-Class' Fantasies: A Neocolonial Analysis of International Branch Campuses. *Organization*, 26: 75–97.

Sirat, M (2008) The Impact of September 11 on International Student Flow into Malaysia: Lessons Learned. *International Journal of Asia Pacific Studies*, 4: 79–95.

Smith, K (2009) Transnational Teaching Experiences: An Under-Explored Territory for Transformative Professional Development. *International Journal for Academic Development*, 14: 111–22.

Smith, K (2010) Assuring Quality in Transnational Higher Education: A Matter of Collaboration or Control? *Studies in Higher Education*, 35: 793–806.

Smith, K (2013) Overseas Flying Faculty Teaching as a Trigger for Transformative Professional Development. *International Journal for Academic Development*, 18: 127–38.

Smith, K (2014) Exploring Flying Faculty Teaching Experiences: Motivations, Challenges and Opportunities. *Studies in Higher Education*, 39: 117–34.

Smith, K (2015) Meeting Expectations: The Challenge of Staff Development with International Collaborative Partners. *Educational Developments*, 16: 11–15.

Smith, K (2017) *Transnational Education Toolkit.* York: Higher Education Academy. [online] Available at: www.heacademy.ac.uk/knowledge-hub/transnational-education-toolkit (accessed 16 January 2020).

Smith, L (2009) Sinking in the Sand? Academic Work in an Offshore Campus of an Australian University. *Higher Education Research and Development*, 28: 467–79.

Spencer-Woods, J E (2020) *A Study of the Tools Used to Overcome Communication and Other Difficulties Encountered by Direct Third Year Entry Chinese Undergraduate Accounting and Finance Students Entering UK Higher Education Directly from the People's Republic of China.* Unpublished EdD thesis, University of Greenwich.

Stella, A (2006) Quality Assurance of Cross-Border Higher Education. *Quality in Higher Education*, 12: 257–76.

Sutrisno, A and Pillay, H (2013) Purposes of Transnational Higher Education Programs: Lessons from Two Indonesian Universities. *Studies in Higher Education*, 38: 1185–200.

Toohey, D, McGill, T and Whitsed, C (2017) Engaging Academic Staff in Transnational Teaching: The Job Satisfaction Challenge. *Journal of Studies in International Education*, 21: 333–48.

Trifiro, F (2019) The Importance of Cross-Border Cooperation in the Quality Assurance of TNE: A Comparative Overview of National Approaches to TNE. *Higher Education Evaluation and Development.*

[online] Available at: www.emerald.com/insight/content/doi/10.1108/HEED-12-2018-0030/full/html (accessed 16 January 2020).

Tsang, E Y-H (2013) The Quest for Higher Education by the Chinese Middle Class: Retrenching Social Mobility? *Studies in Higher Education*, 66: 653–68.

UNESCO/Council of Europe (2000) *Code of Practice in the Provision of Transnational Education.* Bucharest: UNESCO/CEPES.

UUKi (2018) *The Scale of UK Higher Education Transnational Education 2015–2016 – Trend Analysis of HESA Data.* London: UUK. [online] Available at: www.universitiesuk.ac.uk/policy-and-analysis/reports/Pages/the-scale-of-UK-higher-education-transnational-education-2015–16.aspx (accessed 16 January 2020).

Vincent-Lancrin, S and Pfotenhauer, S (2012) *Guidelines for Quality Provision in Cross-Border Higher Education: Where Do We Stand?* Paris: OECD. [online] Available at: www.oecd.org/innovation/research/49956210.pdf (accessed 16 January 2020).

Waters, J and Leung, M (2012) Young People and Reproduction of Disadvantage Through Transnational Education. *Sociological Research Online*, 17. [online] Available at: https://journals.sagepub.com/doi/full/10.5153/sro.2499 (accessed 16 January 2020).

Waters, J and Leung, M (2013) Immobile Transnationalisms? Young People and Their In Situ Experiences of 'International' Education in Hong Kong. *Urban Studies*, 50: 606–20.

Waters, J L and Leung, M (2017) Trans-Knowledge? Geography, Mobility, and Knowledge in Transnational Education. In Jöns, H, Meusburger, P and Heffernan, M (eds) *Mobilities of Knowledge* (pp 269–85). Cham Switzerland: SpringerOpen.

Waterval, G J, Frambach, J M, Driessen, E W and Scherpbier, A J J A (2015) Copy Not Paste: A Literature Review of Crossborder Curriculum Partnerships. *Journal of Studies in International Education*, 19: 65–85.

Weaver, G R (1986) Understanding and Coping with Cross-Cultural Adjustment Stress. In Paige, R M (ed) *Cross-Cultural Orientation: New Conceptualizations and Applications* (pp 111–46). Lanham, MD: University Press of America.

WECD/UUKi (2018) *Transnational Education: Global Location, Local Innovation.* London: UUKi. [online] Available at: www.universitiesuk.ac.uk/policy-and-analysis/reports/Pages/Transnational-education-.aspx (accessed 16 January 2020).

Wilkins, S (2017) Ethical Issues in Transnational Higher Education: The Case of International Branch Campuses. *Studies in Higher Education*, 42: 1385–400.

Wilkins, S and Huisman, J (2012) The International Branch Campus as Transnational Strategy in Higher Education. *Higher Education*, 64: 627–45.

Wilkins, S and Huisman, J (2013) Student Evaluation of University Image Attractiveness and Its Impact on Student Attachment to International Branch Campuses. *Journal of Studies in International Education*, 17: 607–23.

Wilkins, S and Urbanovič, J (2014) English as the Lingua Franca in Transnational Higher Education: Motives and Prospects of Institutions That Teach in Languages Other than English. *Journal of Studies in International Education*, 18: 405–25.

Wilkins, S and Neri, S (2019) Managing Faculty in Transnational Higher Education: Expatriate Academics at International Branch Campuses. *Journal of Studies in International Education*, 23: 451–72.

Wilkinson, E (2015) Technology: The Silent Partner in Transnational Education. *University World News*, 13 February. [online] Available at: www.universityworldnews.com/post.php?story=20150212104813155 (accessed 16 January 2020).

Williams, R A (2018) Sorry We Have No Branch Campuses. *Times Higher Education*, 1 September. [online] Available at: www.timeshighereducation.com/blog/sorry-we-have-no-branch-campuses (accessed 16 January 2020).

Williams, R M (2018) *Quality Assurance in Transnational Education.* Unpublished DBA thesis, University of Bath.

Woodhouse, D (1999) Quality and Quality Assurance. In de Wit, H and Knight, J (eds) *Quality and Internationalisation in Higher Education* (pp. 29–49). Paris: OECD.

WTO [World Trade Organisation] (nd) *The General Agreement on Trade in Services (GATS): Objectives, Coverage and Disciplines.* [online] Available at: www.wto.org/english/tratop_e/serv_e/gatsqa_e.htm (accessed 16 January 2020).

Yokoyama, K (2011) Quality Assurance and the Changing Meaning of Autonomy Between Home and Overseas Campuses of the Universities in New York State. *Journal of Studies in International Education*, 15: 261–78.

Ziguras, C and McBurnie, G (2008) The Impact of Trade Liberalization on Transnational Education. In Dunn, L and Wallace, M (eds) *Teaching in Transnational Higher Education* (pp. 3–13). London: Routledge.

Index